A Mathematical Jamboree

Brian Bolt

CAMBRIDGE
UNIVERSITY PRESS

Published by the Press Syndicate of the University of Cambridge
The Pitt Building, Trumpington Street, Cambridge CB2 1RP
40 West 20th Street, New York, NY 10011–4211, USA
10 Stamford Road, Oakleigh, Melbourne 3166, Australia

First published 1995

ACZ—8246

A catalogue record for this book is available from the British Library

Library of Congress cataloguing in publication data
Bolt, Brian.
A mathematical jamboree / by Brian Bolt   QA
    p.   cm.   95
ISBN 0 521 48589 4 (pbk.)   .B565
1. Mathematical recreations. I. Title.   1995
QA95.B565   1995
793.7'4--dc20   95–12764   CIP

ISBN 0 521 48589 4

Cover illustration and cartoons by Tony Hall
Text illustrations by Peter Welford, Cathryn Willis

Printed in Great Britain by Scotprint Ltd, Musselburgh

Also by this author

Mathematical Activities
More Mathematical Activities
Even More Mathematical Activities
Mathematics Meets Technology
101 Mathematical Projects (with David Hobbs)3

HM

CONTENTS

Page numbers in **bold** refer to the activities.
The second page number refers to the commentary.

INTRODUCTION

Mathematical puzzles have interested me for most of my life and probably stimulated me to more mathematical activity than the conventional mathematical courses by which I earned my living. But having said that, most mathematical puzzles, games and tricks grow out of the properties of number and shape which are at the heart of the subject. Solving the puzzles requires the solver to come to terms with these properties, and in so doing enriches their insight into the intriguing nature of mathematics.

This book is the fifth in this series, each filled with new ideas to challenge the puzzler. It continues with the usual mix of activities from matchsticks to matrices, with a plethora of magical configurations to engage the attention. For the traditional geometer there is a 'proof' that all triangles are isosceles and a deceptively simple figure where you are challenged to find a missing angle. Would-be managers can test out their shunting skills, or organise an expedition of explorers into the interior or minimise transport costs, while pilots can go formation flying with the Red Arrows. A section on ways of making harmonographs will encourage readers with a practical bent to make their own and enjoy the resulting patterns, while the numerous games and tricks can be tried out on your friends.

The puzzles in this book do not normally require a high degree of mathematical knowledge to solve, rather a mixture of insight and tenacity. But whether you succeed or fail, the commentary at the end will make interesting reading and add to your understanding.

My thanks are due to the encouragement I get from correspondents around the world, and the positive feedback from lectures I give to groups of all ages. Special thanks are due to Kate Gentles of Cambridge University Press for her helpful comments and encouragement. Also to my wife, who waits patiently for those DIY jobs to be done when I shut myself away in my study to write!

Brian Bolt

1 Complete the cube

The solid shown can be thought of as being made from four unit cubes.

What is the smallest single solid shape which could be fitted together with the given shape to form a cube?

2 Jasmine's friends

Mrs Jones went to the local greengrocer to buy some fruit for her daughter Jasmine and her friends to refresh them as they took part in a sponsored walk. She bought apples at 4p each and oranges at 7p each, and had 1p change from £3. Jasmine and her friends each had an equal share of the fruit.

How many friends did Jasmine have for company on the walk, and how many apples and oranges did they each have?

3 Building to order!

A prestigious housing estate is planned to have nine detached houses equally spaced in a square 3 × 3 array.

The first house to be built is to be on the NW corner plot of the site, while the last is to be on the SE corner plot.

The building of a new house is only begun when the previous house is completed. The builder builds the next house in such a way that it is not on a plot directly to the north, south, east or west of the one just completed. In how may different ways can the builder order the building of the houses on the nine plots?

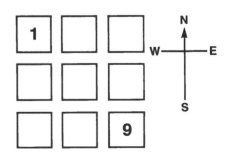

4 Matchstick mansions

What is the smallest number of matches you need to move
to convert the first house into each of the others?

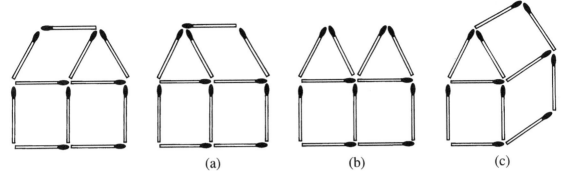

(a)   (b)   (c)

5 Make 24

Ms Challenger asked her class if they could make up a
sum using the same digit just three times, and any
mathematical symbol they liked, to make 24.

Jason Noall had his hand up almost before the question
was finished:

It's easy miss, $8 + 8 + 8 = 24$

Ms Challenger accepted his answer as a good start, and
wrote it up on the board, but suggested there were more
interesting solutions to be found.

Rebecca and Ali worked together quietly in a corner of
the classroom and said nothing until the end of the lesson
when they were able to give four further solutions, each
using a different digit.

How many solutions can you find?

6 Symbolic interpretations!

> ## FIVE PLUS SIX PLUS SEVEN = EIGHTEEN

Delete seven letters from this question so that the equation
remaining is still correct.

Good! Now remove twelve more letters so that what
remains still gives a correct equation.

7 Sort out the symbols!

In this 4 × 4 array each symbol stands for a different number. The sum of the symbols in three of the rows and three of the columns is given. What are the two missing totals?

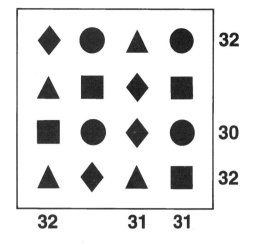

8 Journeying to St Ives!

As I was going to St Ives,
I met a man with seven wives.
Every wife had seven sacks,
Every sack had seven cats,
Every cat had seven kits.
Kits, cats, sacks and wives,
How many were going to St Ives?

This is an old English rhyme based on a puzzle set by Fibonacci in the early part of the thirteenth century in his book, *Liber Abaci*.

9 Punishing perambulations!

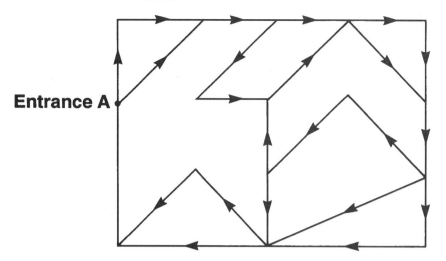

Entrance A

The National Horticultural Society was very proud of its exhibition gardens and it laid out paths for visitors to come and see all their specimen plants. The paths were quite narrow, so, to avoid congestion, they were all carefully marked with arrows to allow only one-way traffic.

Each visitor was given a copy of this map, showing the layout of the paths and the direction they must take along each one. The visitors enter and leave the gardens at *A*. How many different ways could a visitor walk around the garden before first returning to *A*?

How many circuits of the garden would a visitor need to make to see all the exhibits?

10 Sale bargains?

Some weeks before the annual sales, the owner of a furniture store increased the prices of some of the suites of furniture by 20%. He hoped this would make them appear more attractive in the coming sales. Then in the sale these suites of furniture were all advertised as '20% off the marked price!'

What kind of bargain is that?

11 Three in a line

David placed eleven counters on a chessboard as shown and challenged his sister Mary to find how many sets of three counters there were which lay on a straight line. Having answered his question correctly, Mary then challenged David to put one more counter on the board in such a way that 4 more sets of three counters lay on a straight line.

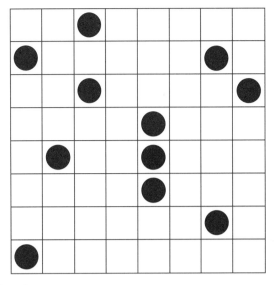

Can you match up to their challenges?

After satisfying each other with their solutions they decided they had the basis of a good game, and spent many hours playing it. What they did was to take some squared paper, mark off an 8 × 8 playing area and take it in turns to shade in a square. Whenever one of them completed a line of three shaded squares they drew a line through it in their colour and claimed a point. No one was allowed to shade a square if it would then form a line of four shaded squares. If one player spotted a line which had been formed by their opponent but not claimed, then they could claim it in their turn before shading another square.

12 Age related!

At their grandmother Elizabeth's birthday celebration, Rosemary and Katherine naturally reflected on their own ages and that of their elders. They soon realised that this was a unique occasion. Katherine's age could be obtained from her older sister Rosemary's age by reversing its digits, while their father James' age was similarly related to grandmother Elizabeth's age. But even more surprising was the fact that the product of Katherine's age and Elizabeth's age was equal to the product of Rosemary's age and James' age. As if this wasn't enough, Katherine is half her father's age and Rosemary is half her grandmother's age.

Now tell me how old they were!

13 Cross out!

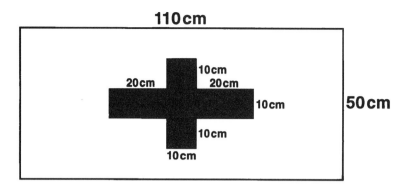

110cm

10cm
20cm **20cm**
10cm
50cm
10cm
10cm

A sheet of metal is in the shape of a rectangle 110 cm long by 50 cm high. A hole has been cut from its centre in the shape of a cross 50 cm long by 30 cm high.

The challenge is to cut it into two identical pieces which fit neatly together to form a rectangle 80 cm by 60 cm high.

Are you up to the challenge?

14 What scores are possible?

2	3	0	4	9	7	8	5	1	6
23	30	04	49	97	78	85	51	16	

A mathematics teacher told her students to write down the digits 0 to 9 in any order they liked, and then to look at the nine two-digit numbers formed by taking each pair of adjacent digits as shown. She told them to score:

1 point for each triangle number
2 points for each square number
3 points for a prime number

In the above example:
78 is triangular, scoring 1 point
04, 49 and 16 are square, scoring 6 points
23 and 97 are prime, scoring 6 points
so this arrangement scores 13 points.

Having understood what was expected of them, they were then challenged to find as high a score as they could by experimenting with different arrangements of the digits.

15 Triangular trios

In how many different ways could you cut out a shape consisting of three adjacent triangles, of which at least one must be black, from this triangular pattern?

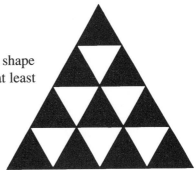

16 Cubical configurations

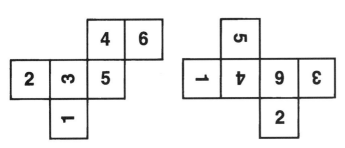

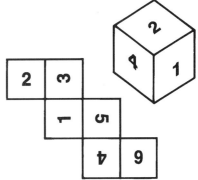

A dice is made in the usual way with the numbers 1 to 6 placed on the faces of a cube so that the numbers on any pair of opposite faces sum to 7. A view of the dice is shown above with three possible nets to make it. Which, if any of these nets is correct? Easy enough to answer if you make the nets and fold them, but are you able to do it without such an aid?

17 Crosswords

Select nine of the ten words shown and place them in a 3 x 3 array so that the three words in every one of the rows, columns and diagonals of the array contain a common letter. Furthermore, if three of the words you have chosen have a letter in common then they must form one of the rows, columns or diagonals of the array.

TAN   SURD   NODE

REAL   LOCI   ADD

TRIO   PLUS   TEST

ISOSCELES

18 Counter change!

This is a solitaire game you can play using two sets of counters on a grid as shown.

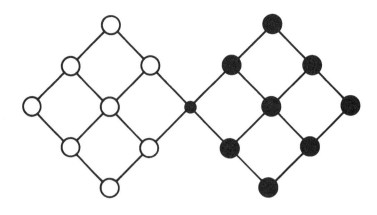

The game starts with the white counters occupying all the intersections on the left of the grid, the black counters occupying all the intersections on the right of the grid and the centre intersection unoccupied.

A white counter can move right to an adjacent unoccupied intersection along one of the diagonals, or by jumping diagonally over a black counter to an unoccupied intersection. The black counters can move in a similar way, but their moves are restricted to left diagonals and jumping over white counters.

The challenge is to find a sequence of moves which will interchange the white counters with the black counters. When you have managed this, the next challenge is to find the smallest number of moves which will bring about the desired interchange. Have fun!

19 All things being equal

	15		7	
6	◯	3	◯	4
	5		2	
12	◯	4	◯	8
	5		6	

Put the signs +, ×, − and ÷ into the circles so that the two computations across and the two vertically give the same result.

20 Safe cracking!

An experienced safe-cracker was hired by a gang to help them get into the large safe at a city bank. He was very experienced at using skeleton keys and the other tools of his trade to crack the most sophisticated locks. But this time he was baffled! The locking mechanism to the safe was controlled by a computer and operated by a battery of press button switches in a 6×4 array. He tried pressing various combinations, sometimes singly, sometimes together, but without success. What he didn't know was that the safe could only be opened if 16 of the switches were pressed in any pattern which had an odd number pressed in each row and column. Armed with this knowledge, could you have opened the safe?

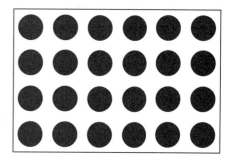

21 Donald's success?

Donald was renowned for his lack of mathematical ability, so when he gave the *correct* answers in a test involving the calculation of the areas of three rectangles his teacher suspected him of cheating. Not wanting to accuse him of this, she invited him to explain how he obtained his answers. Now the one mathematical technique that Donald had mastered was how to add together two numbers correctly, so faced with a question giving two numbers, the length and the breadth, he added them together. Checking the questions she had set, the teacher was astounded to find that in each case the numerical value of the sum of the length and breadth of each rectangle was equal to their product! The areas of the rectangles are given above; what are their dimensions?

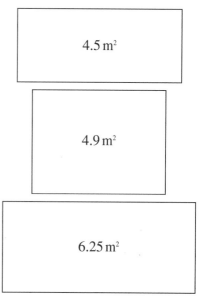

4.5 m²

4.9 m²

6.25 m²

22 Manufacturing squares!

Twelve matches have been arranged as shown to make 3 identical squares.

Show how you can move three matches to make an arrangement with: (a) 5 squares, (b) 7 squares.

How many matches do you need to move to make an arrangement with 6 squares identical in size to the original?

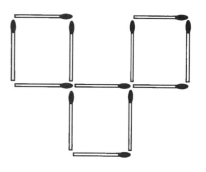

23 Motorway machinations!

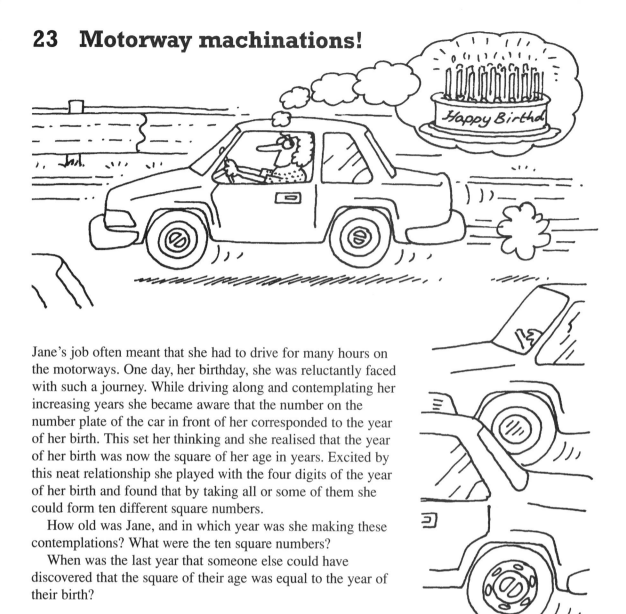

Jane's job often meant that she had to drive for many hours on the motorways. One day, her birthday, she was reluctantly faced with such a journey. While driving along and contemplating her increasing years she became aware that the number on the number plate of the car in front of her corresponded to the year of her birth. This set her thinking and she realised that the year of her birth was now the square of her age in years. Excited by this neat relationship she played with the four digits of the year of her birth and found that by taking all or some of them she could form ten different square numbers.

How old was Jane, and in which year was she making these contemplations? What were the ten square numbers?

When was the last year that someone else could have discovered that the square of their age was equal to the year of their birth?

24 Turn about!

$23 \times 96 = 32 \times 69$

Now I don't suppose many readers carry this unusual number relationship in their head, or have ever met it before. But surprisingly there are several such pairs of two-digit numbers where their product stays the same when the order of the digits is reversed.

How many can you find? Investigate!

25 The open prison!

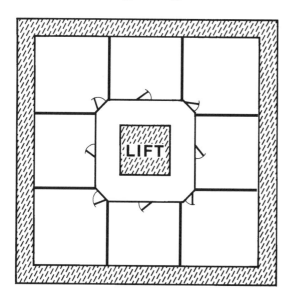

A new open prison had its cells arranged eight to a floor on the sides of a square tower block, as shown, so there were three cells along each wall. Each cell had 3 prisoners allocated to it giving a total of 24 prisoners to each floor. Now on any particular floor the prisoners were allowed to associate freely with the other prisoners along the same wall as themselves, so that at any given time the number of prisoners in a cell could differ from 3. However, the warders decided they could easily keep a check on their charges by shutting the cell doors on the hour and ensuring that there were a total of 9 prisoners in the three cells along each wall. The prisoners soon realised there was a flaw in this counting system and exploited it to their advantage!

On Friday after exercising in the prison yard 4 of the prisoners slipped over the boundary wall and made their escape for a long weekend at home. When the warders made their count back in the cells they suspected nothing amiss as there were still 9 prisoners in the cell along each wall.

The missing prisoners returned on Monday, along with 4 of their friends who wanted to sample the prison amenities, slipping surreptitiously over the boundary wall to join the other inmates in the exercise yard. Returning to their cells they found no problem in again fooling their warders, who found 9 prisoners in the cells on each of the four walls.

How could the prisoners have fooled their warders? See how many essentially different solutions you can find.

26 Ayesha's offcuts

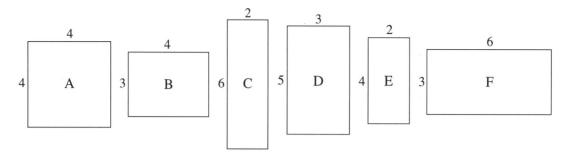

Ayesha's father was a builder and often brought home offcuts of wood from his latest job to burn on the fire. One winter's night his offcuts included six rectangular pieces of plywood as shown. Now Ayesha liked doing jigsaws and soon started playing with the pieces to see what shapes she could make.

In a very short time she discovered, to her pleasure, she could make a square using all the pieces. She wondered whether she had been lucky to arrive at the square so quickly, and decided to see if there were other arrangements of the six rectangles which would also make the square. She quickly found several, so she decided to label the pieces A, B, C, D, E, F and record her solutions on squared paper.

How many distinct solutions can you find?

Ayesha found one solution without a fault line, which particularly pleased her. Can you find it?

(A fault line is a straight line between the pieces which goes right across the square.)

27 A triple prime!

The three digit number **XYZ** is such that **X**, **Y** and **Z** are different primes and the number is divisible by each of them. What is the number?

28 Coin magic

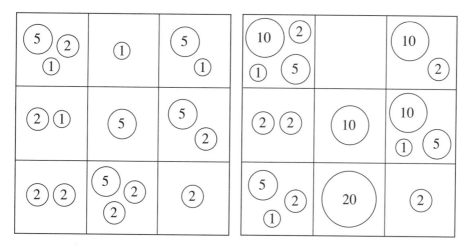

The magician intrigued his audience by placing coins on the nine squares of a 3 × 3 array so that the totals of the coins in each row, column and diagonal were equal, and the value of the coins in each of the squares was different. He was using British coins, which come in values of 1p, 2p, 5p, 10p, 20p, 50p and 100p. Two of his examples are shown, each requiring 17 coins and giving magic squares with magic totals of 15 and 30 respectively. He then took just twelve coins and formed a similar magic square. What coins did he use?

29 Mustafa's mosaics

Sheik Abdul Aziz Mustafa, like most of his compatriots, was fascinated by mosaic patterns, and he also had a great belief that all the good luck in his family was associated with the number 13. So when he wanted to build a new palace he held a competition inviting architects to submit designs to incorporate as many different square mosaic patterns as possible. But he stipulated that each pattern should consist of just 13 square mosaic tiles, tiles which were only available in three sizes: 1 × 1, 2 × 2 and 3 × 3.

How many designs would you have found if you had been the architect?

30 Lord Fearful's fortifications

Lord Fearful had inherited many priceless treasures from a long line of ancestors so, anxious to protect them, he built a complicated set of walled fortifications around his castle. These consisted of six sets of battlemented walls, each in the form of a square, placed inside each other so that the mid-points of the sides of one square formed the corners of the next. At the corner of each square there was a lookout tower, which contained accommodation for his many guards. Now the number of guards he housed in each tower was determined by a very simple rule.

If there are m guards in a tower at one corner of a square, and n guards in an adjacent corner of the square then the number of guards in the tower between them is the numerical difference in m and n.

The second diagram illustrates this with three squares.

Now the largest number of guards Lord Fearful had in a tower was 37, and these were in a corner of the largest square. In the opposite corner of this square were 11 guards, while the sixth and smallest square housed 4, 4, 8 and 16 guards respectively.

How many guards did Lord Fearful have in his 24 towers altogether, and how were they distributed?

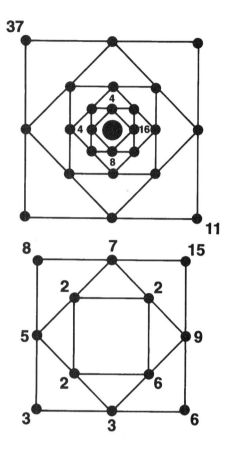

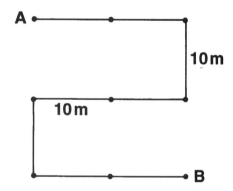

31 Norman's radio aerial

My next-door neighbour Norman is a keen radio ham, and through his radio transmissions he has friends all over the world. To improve his radio reception he is forever experimenting with his aerial, which he attaches to the top of nine tall masts placed in a square 3 x 3 pattern as shown where the masts are 10 m apart. His current aerial follows the rectangular path shown from A to B with a total length of 80 m. He wants to increase the length of the aerial using the same masts, but it still needs to start at A and end at B, meeting each of the other masts once on the way.

Investigate possible routes for the aerial and find the longest aerial he can manage if:
(a) the aerial does not cross over itself,
(b) the aerial is allowed to cross itself.

32 The three dice trick

Ask someone to roll three dice on a table without you
looking and to add up all the dots on their top faces. Next
they are to choose one of the dice and add in the number
of dots on its bottom face to the total already found.
Finally, the person is invited to roll the chosen dice
a second time and to add in the total on its new
top face. By looking at the dice in their final
positions you can quickly give the total found! How?

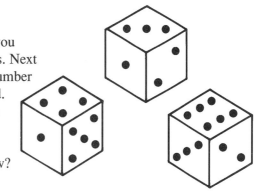

33 The scouts' initiative test!

A scout was stood on each of three barrels placed at the
vertices of an equilateral triangle, a distance 3 metres apart.

They were told to imagine that they were surrounded by
crocodile-infested waters and had to find some way of
transferring themselves from one barrel to another. To help
them in this enterprise they each had a floorboard of length
2.5 metres. How could they safely bridge the gap?

34 The rugger tournament

In a local five-a-side rugger tournament the three schools teams, Avengers, Bashers and Corruptibles, each played each other once. A young reporter on his first assignment wrote down the match details on the proforma shown here. But when he returned to the office he found, to his consternation, that the lavish entertainment in the

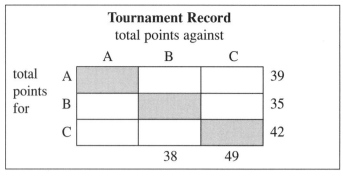

		Tournament Record total points against			
		A	B	C	
total points for	A				39
	B				35
	C				42
			38	49	

clubhouse after the matches resulted in drink being spilled on his match data, so that most of it was illegible. He did recall that one match was drawn and eventually managed to deduce all the missing facts from the data still visible.

Can you deduce the scores of all the matches from the above data?

35 Do your eyes deceive you?

How good are we at judging lengths and areas? Surely $CD > AB$ in (i) and $PQ > QR$ in (ii). And how about AB and BC in (iii)? There is no doubt that the shaded region in the centre of the square has a larger area than the outside border … or is there? Which of the soldiers in (v) is the tallest? Our eyes are easily fooled by the context of the parts of a drawing, but in all of these examples the parts compared are equal.

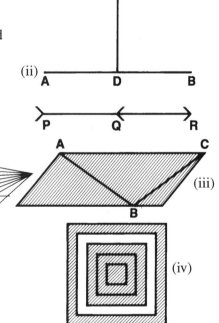

22

36 A cubical crawl

A spider can crawl around the base of a large cubical crate in 4 minutes. How long would it take to crawl, at the same speed, from the bottom corner at *A* to the opposite corner at *B* if it chooses a shortest route?

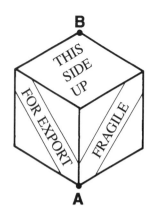

37 Only 'takes' and 'adds'

1 2 3 4 5 6 7 8 9

Many different totals can be achieved by inserting only '+' and '–' signs between some or all of the digits 1 to 9 in order.
For example:

$1 + 2 + 3 + 4 - 5 + 6 + 7 - 8 - 9 = 1$
$123 - 4 - 5 - 6 - 7 + 8 - 9 = 100$

How many of the totals between 1 and 100 can you achieve?

38 Striking the hour

A clock takes three seconds to strike 3 o'clock. How long does it take to strike 6 o'clock?

39 A frog he would a-wooing go!

A frog spent most of his time in a pond in the corner of a small urban garden, but when the mating season arrived he did a tour of the garden jumping from one paving slab to the next in search of a mate. The frog only jumped parallel to the paving slabs, never diagonally, and avoids the flower beds altogether.

Show that the frog can visit each paving slab once only and return to the pond.

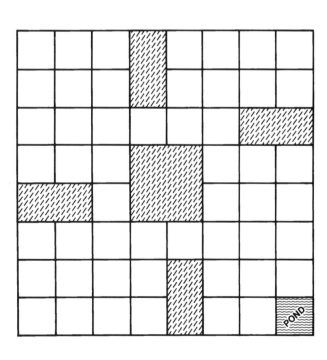

40 A fishy connection!

Show how to cut the square into three pieces which will fit together to form the fish ... or, if you prefer, cut the fish into three pieces which will fit together to form the square!

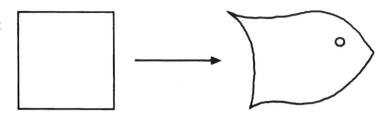

41 Pool-ball triangles

Many years ago now, George Sicherman from New York was watching the 15 balls being set up in a triangular array at the start of a game of pool. The balls are numbered 1 to 15, and it occurred to him that it might be possible to arrange them in such a way that the number on any particular ball is equal to the difference between the numbers on the two balls which it touches above. Well this can be done, but before tackling that problem try yourself out on the following easier problems.

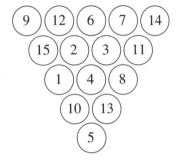

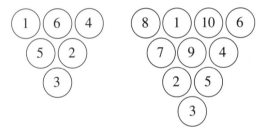

The diagram shows two arrangements of pool balls satisfying George Sicherman's criteria for:

(a) the balls numbered 1 to 6,
(b) the balls numbered 1 to 10.

In each case there are three further solutions for you to find.

When you have found these you will be ready to tackle the original 15-ball problem. Good luck!

42 Magic squares to magic tetrahedra

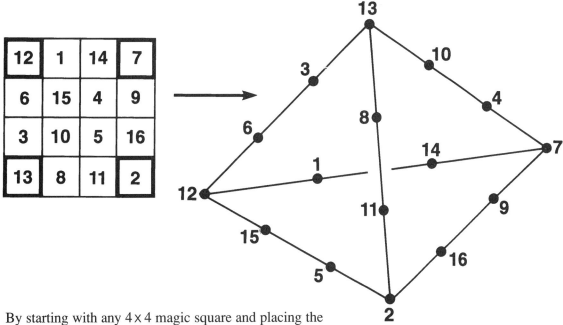

12	1	14	7
6	15	4	9
3	10	5	16
13	8	11	2

By starting with any 4×4 magic square and placing the four numbers from its corners at the vertices of a tetrahedron it is then an easy matter to place the remaining twelve numbers, two at a time, along its six edges so that the total along each edge is the same. In the example above, the numbers 1 to 16 are used and the magic total is 34.

Having formed the magic tetrahedron in this way, $2^6 = 64$ different magic tetrahedra can be formed by interchanging the orders of the pairs of numbers in the middle of each edge, all with 2, 7, 12 and 13 at their vertices. But having made such a change don't imagine you can transform back to give a different magic square!

Now place 1 to 16 on the tetrahedron with 3, 6, 10 and 15 at its vertices to make it magic.

43 All ten digits!

The number **PQQQQ** when squared is 1 more than a number which contains each of the digits 0, 1, 2, ... ,9. What is it?

44 By a whisker!

A mouse was contentedly nibbling a piece of cheese by the wall at the foot of the staircase at A (see the diagram) when a cat appeared at the top of the stairs. Seeing danger, the mouse ran for its life to its hole which was at B, on the fourth stair on the opposite side of the staircase. Now the stairs are 100 cm wide, the treads measure 20 cm from front to back, and the risers are 15 cm high. The cat was slow to react, but reached the hole with one mighty bound, 3 seconds after the mouse started its home run. Now the mouse, when frightened, can run at 60 cm/s. Who won the race to the hole?

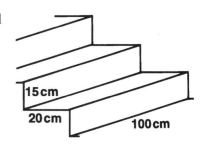

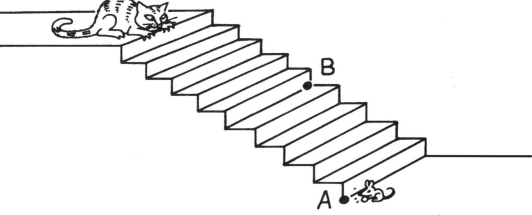

45 Pythagorean perimeters!

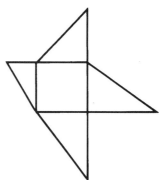

A large Australian cattle ranch can best be described as having the shape of a square, on each of whose sides there is a right-angled triangle. Now all the triangles are different in size, but have the property that their sides are all a whole number of kilometres in length.

What is the shortest possible perimeter of the ranch?

46 Magic circles

The six circles shown each pass through four of the eight black spots in the figure. Allocate the numbers 1, 2, ... ,8 to the spots in such a way that the total of the four numbers on each circle is the same.

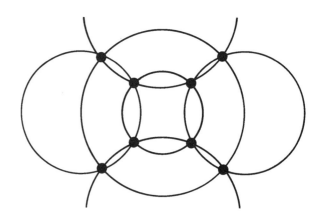

47 Armchair football

Twinkle Toes had been a footballer of some note in his youth, but now his interest was mainly conducted from an armchair watching television. He regularly did the football pools, hoping to win a fortune, and religiously watched the Saturday programme giving all the day's results. One day after an outstanding 5-3 win by his favourite team, Manchester United, he got around to wondering:

(a) what the score might have been at half time; was it, for example, 0–0, or 1–3, or 4–2, or what?
(b) in how many different ways might the score have progressed from 0–0 to 5–3?

His long experience of the game made him realise there would be several possibilities, and he eventually arrived at an answer for each after much scribbling around the edges of his newspaper.

How many half-time scores were possible, and in how many ways could the score have progressed from 0–0 to 5–3?

Can you generalise your findings?

48 Commercialising Catch!

While doing a Saturday job at their local Supermarket, Ruth and Susan were asked to create a display to promote CATCH, a new brand of cat food. The manager gave them a large number of CATCH cans and they set about building a wall with them in such a way that each new layer had one fewer cans than the layer below. With the number of cans they were given they were surprised to find they could build the wall in five different ways, depending on the number of cans they put in the bottom layer, each way using all the cans. When they had finished, the manager inquired of them how many cans they had used. Ruth, who had been counting as they went along, thought there were 128, but Sally made a calculation based on the number of cans in the top and bottom layers of their final arrangement and thought the number was 126.

Assuming that one of them was correct, how many cans were there, and how many would there have been in the top layer of the tallest wall they built?

49   Squaring squares!

Squares can be subdivided into non-overlapping squares in many ways. For which values of N is it possible to divide a square into N non-overlapping squares?

50   Seasonal visiting

At New Year, Raheem always spent one day of his holiday visiting his many relatives who lived in the villages labelled A to J on the map. Raheem lived at A, and the map shows all the available roads he could take to his relatives with the distances along them in kilometres. To limit the distance he had to travel Raheem used the nearest village strategy, that is he always travelled to the nearest village to where he then was that he had not already visited. What was

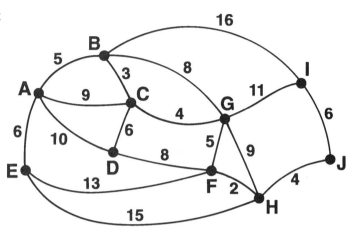

Raheem's route, and how far did he have to travel before getting back to his home at A again?

What is the shortest journey Raheem could make to visit all his relatives?

51   Lunar areas

Semicircles are drawn on each side of a right-angled triangle ABC, as shown in the diagram. The semicircle on the hypotenuse AB of the triangle overlaps parts of the other two semicircles leaving two lunes, shaded above. How is the area formed by the two lunes, taken together, related to the area of the triangle?

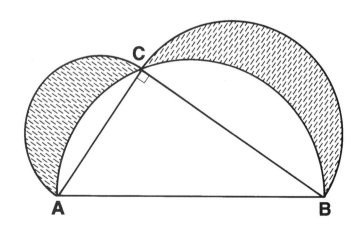

52 Cable connections

	A	B	C	D	E	F
A		7	15	8	8	20
B			10	5	11	14
C				9	13	4
D					6	12
E						16

The Much Talk Telephone Company want to interconnect the towns A, B, C, D, E and F by new efficient fibreglass cables. These are to be put underground and the existing ugly overhead wires replaced. But cutting trenches along the roads to bury the cables is expensive, so it is important that the towns are interconnected in such a way that the length of trench is minimised. The table above gives the lengths of the roads which may be used between the towns, measured in kilometres.

What is the minimum length of trench required?

Where should the company build their new telephone exchange if they want to keep its distance from each of the towns as small as possible?

53 A matter of relative speed!

Jenny and her cousin Jonathan were keen rowers who lived on the bank of a tidal estuary. Rowing downstream with the current, as the tide was going out, Jenny could reach her cousin's landing stage in 10 minutes. But if Jonathan had rowed against the current to Jenny he would have taken 30 minutes even though he rowed at the same speed as Jenny. How long would either of them have taken to row to the other at slack water (that is, when there was no current) if they rowed at the same speed?

If they had both set out to row towards each other when the tide was going out, how long would it be before they met?

54 Party politics!

In planning her daughter Yasmin's fourteenth birthday party Mrs Medalalot suggested to Yasmin that she invite four girls and five boys. As she wanted the party to be as happy an affair as possible, and many of the games involved pairing off the boys with the girls, she devised a plan to bring this about. Each boy was given a list of the girls and asked, in confidence, to give each of them a mark out of ten which represented how they would view having them as a partner for the party games. The result of this exercise is shown in the table below. It quickly became apparent to Mrs Medalalot that Zoe was every boy's first choice, but she did the best she could by pairing off the boys with the girls to maximise the total 'feel good' factor.

Who was paired with whom? Which boy felt most aggrieved?

It isn't recorded what the girls thought of this arrangement. That is left to your imagination!

	Anna	Emma	Yasmin	Karen	Zoe
Akram	6	4	8	6	9
Chris	7	5	5	4	8
Eric	5	6	7	7	10
Martin	4	8	9	5	9
Roger	8	5	7	4	10

55 Bridge building?

Four rods AB, BC, CD, and DA are bolted together at their ends. AB is of length 200 cm, AD and BC of length 60 cm and DC of length 80 cm. It is required to add two rods from D and C to the middle point, M, of AB to strengthen the structure. How long

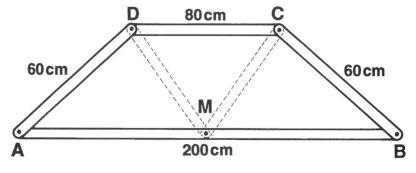

56 Formation flying

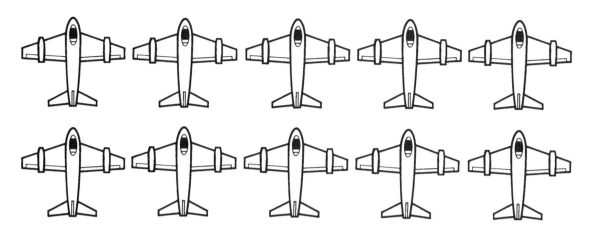

The leader of the Red Arrows display team was always looking
for new formations to show off the flying skills of his team at
their public displays all over the world. After one brain-
storming session he came up with a way to change from a
pattern of two rows of 5 planes to a pattern in which there were
five lines each containing 4 planes. The change of formation
was achieved by only 4 planes changing their positions relative
to the other 6 planes who held formation. Which planes
changed position relative to the others and what was their new
formation?

57 The robotic mouse!

A robotic mouse is given a
program and let loose. The
first 20 legs of its journey are
shown below, where its first
leg is to travel 2 metres in a
northerly direction. Where
will it be in relation to its
starting point when it next
makes a right turn?

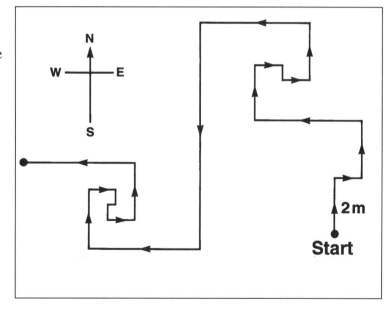

58 Finding the centre

The carpenter had carefully cut out four circular wooden discs which he was going to use as wheels for a toy. His next task was to find the centre of each disc so that he could drill a hole for the axle. But the only tools he had to hand were a set square and a pencil. How could he use these to accurately determine the centre of each wheel?

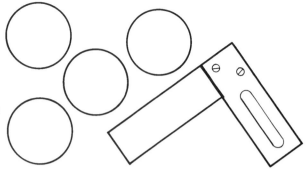

59 Number wheels!

The six-spoked wheel shown has nineteen circles placed symmetrically on it, so that each spoke and each section of the rim contains three of them. The challenge is to find ways of placing the numbers 1 to 19 in the circles so that the total along each spoke and section of rim is the same. One solution is partially completed to give you a flying start, but there are many more. How many can you find?

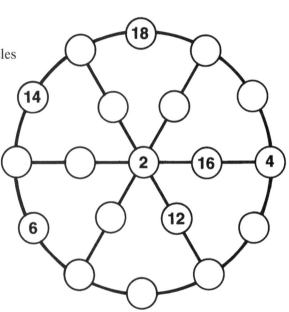

60 Equal products!

$$
\begin{array}{r}
158 \\
\times\ \ 23 \\
\hline
3634
\end{array}
\qquad
\begin{array}{r}
79 \\
\times\ 46 \\
\hline
3634
\end{array}
$$

Isla enjoyed her maths lessons and was rapidly working through an exercise of multiplications when she noticed that two of her answers were the same. This interested her, but on further inspection she was intrigued to find that the two products between them used up each of the digits 1 to 9. Fascinated, she abandoned the exercise in order to see if other similar products could be found, that is:

$abc \times de = fg \times hi$

Where the letters stand for 1 to 9 in some order.
   What is the largest result of such products?

61 More insights into magic squares

Take any five numbers a, b, c, d, and e and put them in the first row of a 5×5 array. Now shift them 3 places to the left for the second row as shown. The following rows are formed by further shifts of 3 places to the left. The resultant then has a, b, c, d, and e in each of the 5 rows, 5 columns and each of the two diagonals so it is magic! Similar arrays constructed by shifts of 2 places are also magic, but a shift of 4 places is not magic. Why?

a	b	c	d	e
d	e	a	b	c
b	c	d	e	a
e	a	b	c	d
c	d	e	a	b

But where does this get us?

Consider the two magic squares below, formed by:

(i) starting with 1, 2, 3, 4, 5, and using a shift of 3 places to the left,

(ii) starting with 0, 5, 10, 15, 20, and using a shift of 2 places to the left.

1	2	3	4	5
4	5	1	2	3
2	3	4	5	1
5	1	2	3	4
3	4	5	1	2

(i)

0	5	10	15	20
10	15	20	0	5
20	0	5	10	15
5	10	15	20	0
15	20	0	5	10

(ii)

1	7	13	19	25
14	20	21	2	8
22	3	9	15	16
10	11	17	23	4
18	24	5	6	12

(iii)

The third square is just formed by adding the corresponding numbers of the first two and contains all the numbers from 1 to 25, giving a magic total of 65. In my earlier books I have described other methods of obtaining a 5×5 magic square containing 1 to 25, but they all give magic squares with 13, the median number, in the middle cell. This time 9 is in the centre which came as something of a surprise. Experimenting further along the above lines you can obtain a variety of 5×5 magic squares containing 1 to 25.

See what you can find!

62 Where is the shopping centre?

The Sellmore grocery chain plan to build a large new out-of-town shopping centre to be sited at S, see the diagram, so that the sum of the distances from it to the three towns Aldwick, Barton and Cowbury is a minimum. The distances between the towns are given in the diagram in kilometres. How far must S be from each of the towns?

Cowbury

10   S   9

Barton   13   Aldwick

63 Negotiating the corridor

Mr and Mrs Social-Climber were moving into a prestigious apartment in a new building development. But on the day of their removal they had a panic for they realised that the only way to their new abode was along a long corridor in which there was a right-angled bend (see the diagram). Would their prize possession, a beautiful antique dining table, negotiate the corridor, let alone the bend? In the event the furniture removals men were able to dismantle the table into two identical pieces, each with three legs, and found they could just manage, even though the table top was held horizontally the whole time.

What was the shape and area of the top of the table given that it was the largest which could negotiate the bend?

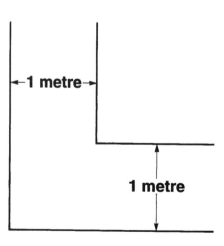

←1 metre→

1 metre

64 Marti's many routes!

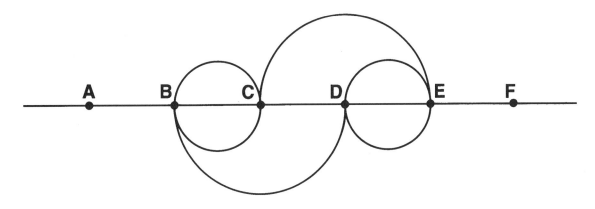

Marti Multivariant was a somewhat eccentric teacher who travelled to school on the underground railway, from station A near her home to station F near her school. To break the monotony of this daily journey she decided to see how many alternative routes she could find along the rail network shown in the above map. Each day she chose a new route, and found to her delight that she was able to find a different one for each day of the academic year before having to repeat herself. Going home at the end of the day she always took the straight route FEDCBA, but her morning journeys to school confused her pupils, who would often catch sight of her travelling along a line away from school!

Now her routes didn't take her over the same line twice, and none of her routes used more than 8 stages, for although many 9 stage routes exist, to use them would have necessitated getting out of bed much earlier. So, how many days did Marti have in her academic year?

65 Fancy that!

The number 2 438 195 760 formed by all ten digits, each used just once, is divisible by all the whole numbers from 1 to 18. What other numbers using all ten digits only once can you find with the same property?

66 Which route to follow?

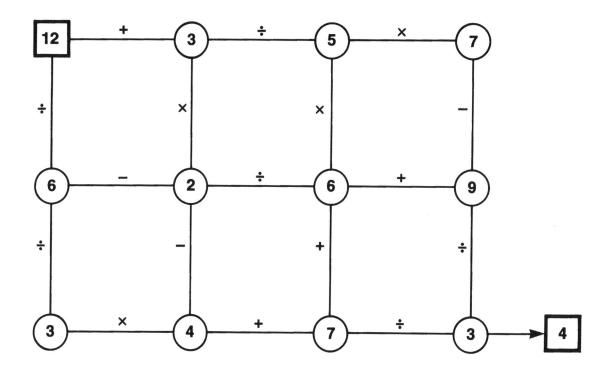

Starting with 12 in the top left-hand corner, find a route
along the network, carrying out the appropriate operations
as you go, which ends in 4 at the bottom right hand corner.
(You cannot go through the same number twice.)

67 Triangular number tiles

Ruth and Roger had a set of triangular tiles in their toybox
numbered 1 to 9, which they fitted together to make
various patterns. One day their mother observed they had
made a large triangle, using all nine tiles, which had the
property that the numbers on the tiles making up the three
triangles composed of four tiles had the same total, 17, as
shown. Intrigued by this, she got out the tiles to play with
when her children had gone to bed and she found many
arrangements of the tiles where the corner triangles had
the same sum. How many arrangements can you find?

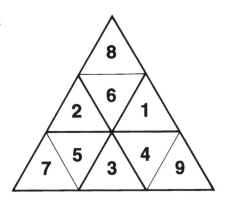

68 Panoramic possibilities!

In my possession I have a set of 24 cards, all of the same size, on each of which is a picture of a landscape. Now they are so designed that no matter which cards are put alongside each other the landscapes fit neatly together. The idea of the cards is to create different panoramic pictures by fitting all the cards side by side.

Now suppose I have worked out a systematic way to generate all the possible panoramic pictures by starting with one panorama and making the minimum number of interchanges at each stage to create a new panoramic picture. If I am slick, my method allows me to create a new panorama, on average, every second. How long will it take me to see all the possible panoramic pictures?

69 Prime magic!

15	113	47
89	59	29
71	5	101

The above magic square with only prime number entries has the lowest possible magic total for such squares ... unless of course you allow some of the prime numbers to be negative. Show that a prime number magic square exists where the magic total is 15.

70 Traffic management

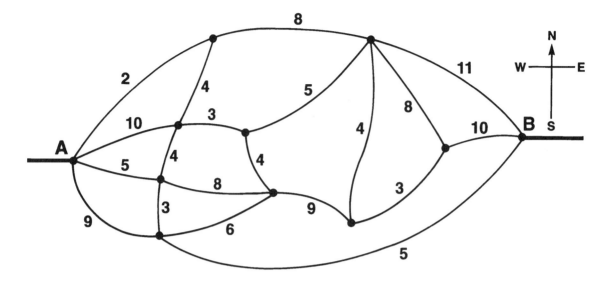

The map shows the streets of a major town. Traffic entering at *A* off the trunk road from the west can make its way through the town in a variety of ways before exiting at *B* onto the trunk road going east. The numbers on each street give the maximum capacity of each street in hundreds of vehicles an hour which can travel along it.

What is the largest number of vehicles an hour which could pass through the town?

71 1089 and the rest!

Take any three-digit number such as 762, which is not symmetric about its middle, form a new three-digit number by reversing the order of its digits, and take the smaller of these numbers from the larger. Now add to this three-digit difference the three-digit number formed by reversing its digits.

In every case the result will be 1089.

This result is well known but how many of you have explored what happens when you do the same with four-digit, five-digit and six-digit numbers? Use your calculator to investigate these larger numbers and see what patterns emerge!

$$\begin{array}{r} -\ 762 \\ 267 \\ \hline +\ 495 \\ 594 \\ \hline 1089 \end{array}$$

72 A magical eye!

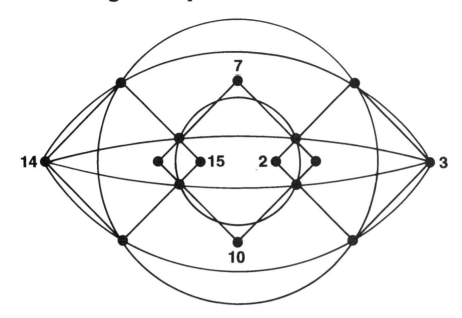

There are, amazingly, many ways of placing the numbers 1 to 16 on the sixteen points indicated on the above figure so that the four numbers:

at the corners of a square,
on a circle,
on a circular arc,

all sum to 34. To give you a start in finding such a solution, six numbers have already been allocated.

73 Devious Diana's dice

Diana enjoyed inventing games to play with her younger brother, Joe. Sometimes, to add spice to the games, they would stake their pocket money on the outcome. One day she invented a very simple game where they each threw a dice, and then calculated the difference between them. Now the difference could be either 0, 1, 2, 3, 4 or 5, so to be fair it was decided that Diana would be declared the winner if the difference was 0, 1 or 2, while Joe would be the winner if the difference was 3, 4 or 5. After a few throws Joe began to lose interest, but then Diana encouraged him by promising to pay him 10p every time he won two consecutive throws as long as he paid her 5p every time she won three consecutive throws. Joe couldn't resist this offer ... but was he wise?

74 Square sisters!

Anthea and her younger sister Ena enjoyed playing with numbers and one day they discussed their ages. Out of interest, Anthea wrote down the factors of her age in years, including 1 and the age itself, added all the factors together and declared she was special as the factors summed to a square number. Not to be outdone, Ena did the same with her own age and was astonished to find that her factors also summed to a square number, exactly the same square number as her sister. How old were they, assuming they were not twins?

75 Shunt your way out of this!

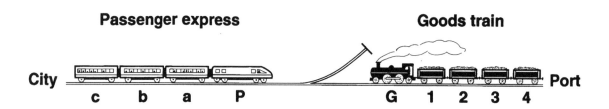

The signalman caused consternation on the single railway track between the city and the port when he allowed a passenger express with three carriages to hurtle towards a slow goods-train hauling four heavily-laden wagons from the port. Thankfully, disaster was averted by the use of warning signals which brought the two trains to a halt just in time to avoid a head-on collision.

The problem now was to decide how best to sort out the situation without one of the trains reversing many miles to their point of departure. Fortunately, there was a short siding at the point where they had halted. It could only be approached from the city direction, and could only hold an engine, or a wagon or a carriage, but it is enough for the experienced engine-drivers to see a way out of their situation. Now the situation is complicated by the fact that the engines can only be coupled to the wagons or carriages at their rear, although these can be coupled to each other at either end.

Can you see how to shunt your way out of this situation so that the two trains pass each other and go happily on their way?

76 Map folding

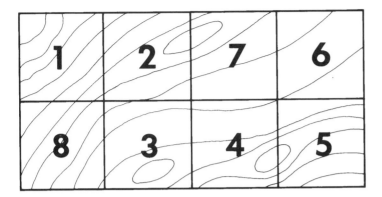

Anyone used to using large Ordnance Survey maps for walking will be aware of the many ways they can be folded to bring the required area into use. The map here has 8 square sections as shown. Can you show how it can be folded so that the eight sections come in the order 1, 2, …, 8, underneath one another with the 1 on top?

Cut out a rectangle of paper to represent the map, mark in the squares and label them with the numbers 1 to 8 as shown – it helps to have both sides labelled – and see what you can do.

77 Spot check!

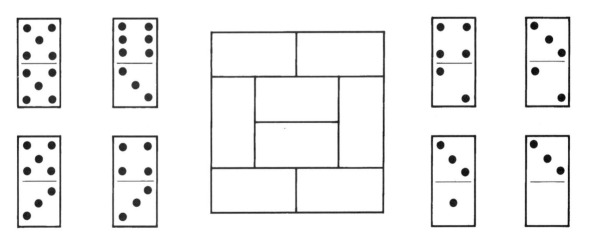

The eight dominoes given above can be fitted into the 4 x 4 square grid shown in such a way that the total number of dots in each of the four rows, four columns, and two diagonals is the same. Can you do it?

78 Neighbourliness!

One wet winter afternoon Jamie became bored with his books and listening to his tapes so he started using his cassette tape boxes like building bricks to design imaginative structures. Then he started thinking about ways of fitting the boxes together, with a fixed number always touching each other (that is, they always had part of a flat face touching). After much juggling around with his boxes he found ways of fitting together six of them so that:

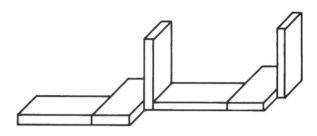

(a) each box touched exactly three others,
(b) each box touched exactly four others,
(c) each box touched exactly five others,

Jamie felt quite smug when he had achieved this and now challenges you to do the same.

Don't be satisfied with one solution, see what different ones are possible!

79 The communicative sisters

Six sisters keep in touch with each other by phone every Sunday evening. When two sisters make contact, they update each other on the news about themselves and about any news gleaned about their other sisters from previous calls that day.

What is the smallest number of phone calls required for all six of the sisters to be updated about each other?

80 Marvellous '26'

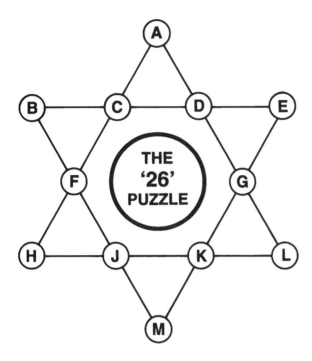

This is an Edwardian board game for one person to play, based on arranging discs numbered 1, 2, 3, …, 12 on a board made from two interlocking triangles as shown. The player has to place the discs to maximise the number of sets in straight lines or other meaningful spatial arrangements which total 26. The notes which came with the puzzle said:

Children would probably make from one to three or four 'twenty sixes' along the sides of the two triangles, but the more advanced operator may make each of the six sides ACFH, ADGL, HJKL, BCDE, BFJM, EGKM as well as the six numbers around the hexagon total '26', with perhaps the finding of several additional twenty sixes. Thus the worker is rewarded or encouraged while in an ordinary puzzle there is entire failure short of entire success. It is possible to show 30 or more sets of '26' in one arrangement, and as there are six entirely different arrangements of these twelve numbers it will be seen that from 100 to 200 different '26s' in legitimate regular forms may be found in this Marvellous '26' puzzle.

See what arrangements you can find to maximise the sets of numbers which total 26.

81 Anna's Christmas shopping

Anna had been shopping in New York for some Christmas presents for her family, and on reaching home she decided to check how much she had spent. She had purchased three presents and had a bill for each so getting out her calculator it was an easy matter for her. However she was careless at first and used the '×' key instead of the '+' key. This gave her a 'total' of 9.96 dollars. Realising her mistake she keyed in the three prices again, but this time correctly used the '+' key. To her amazement her calculator gave the same answer, 9.96 dollars! She repeated both sets of calculations several times, and then was quite excited that she had selected three purchases whose prices had this unusual relationship.

What were the individual prices of Anna's purchase?

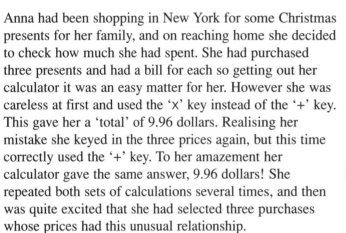

82 Alphabetic arithmetic!

Find the smallest positive integer a for which the following set of equations can be satisfied where every letter stands for a different positive integer less than 1000.

$$\frac{1}{a} = \frac{1}{b} + \frac{1}{c} = \frac{1}{d} + \frac{1}{e} = \frac{1}{f} + \frac{1}{g}$$
$$= \frac{1}{h} + \frac{1}{i} + \frac{1}{j} = \frac{1}{k} + \frac{1}{l} + \frac{1}{m}$$
$$= \frac{1}{n} + \frac{1}{p} + \frac{1}{q} = \frac{1}{r} + \frac{1}{s} + \frac{1}{t}$$
$$= \frac{1}{u} + \frac{1}{v} + \frac{1}{w} = \frac{1}{x} + \frac{1}{y} + \frac{1}{z}$$

83 Who won?

In an athletics match between Athlone College and Barchester High School there were just 8 events and 2 competitors from each school in each event. The resulting positions obtained by the schools in the overall match are given in the table:

Position	1st	2nd	3rd	4th
Athlone	6	0	4	6
Barchester	2	8	4	2

Who do you think should be declared the match winners?

In inter-school matches of this kind, various scoring systems are used and the following are three such, where the points given for a position in each event are shown. For example, a first place in system X scores 5 points, a second scores 3, a third scores 2 and a fourth scores 1.

Position	1st	2nd	3rd	4th
system X	5	3	2	1
system Y	3	2	1	0
system Z	6	3	2	1

Each of these systems have plausible arguments to support them, and you may have your preference.

Work out the points total for each team using each of the scoring systems. What do you deduce?

84 How old are they?

Reversing the digits of grandfather Arthur's age gives that of his son Brian. The difference of their ages is three times that of Arthur's grandson Christopher, which in turn is a seventh of his grandfather's age. Neither Arthur nor Brian were teenage fathers.

How old are they?

85 In-flight refuelling

A jet fighter has a maximum range of 2000 miles on full fuel tanks, but it can be refuelled in flight by a tanker aircraft which can carry fuel sufficient for 8400 fighter miles or 4200 tanker miles. The fuel is stored in a tanker in such a way that it can be used by a tanker itself or for refuelling up to two other planes at a time. Tankers can refuel each other as well as fighter planes, but always need to retain sufficient fuel to return to the base they share with their fighters.

How far could a fighter fly from its base to a distant aircraft carrier if it takes off with full tanks accompanied by two tanker aircraft also with full tanks?

86 All scores equal!

A dart board has four regions as shown, with the centre circle valued at 11, and the rings valued at 7, 3 and 2 as you move further from the centre. One day Alan, Ben, Cheryl and Denise were playing, and after they had each thrown 6 darts they all had the same total score, although they had achieved it in different ways. Alan had the most darts in the centre, Denise was the most consistent, while Ben's darts were evenly spread in the regions he used.

What was their common score and how did each of them achieve it?

87 The dinner party

Four married couples went out to dinner together on a regular
basis, and over the years they had contrived a set of rules for the
order in which they sat around the round table at the restaurant.
Men and women alternated, and no one sat next to or opposite
their partner. Mr Drab and Mrs Allnight were twins who did their
best to avoid each other, while Mr Bright and Mrs Colourful
were rather fond of each other and liked to sit beside one another
whenever possible. Otherwise they were all happy with whom
they sat beside. In what order should they sit around the table?

88 Mind reading!

Give someone a calculator and ask them to key in any five-digit
number. Ask them to multiply the number by 10 and then
subtract the original number. Now get them to add 234 to the
result and give you all but one of the digits of the result,
repeating digits if necessary. Within seconds you will be able to
give the missing digit! But how? All you have to do is add
together the digits you are given and to take them away from the
nearest multiple of 9 above their sum. The difference gives the
required missing digit!

For example, a person keys in 35 241, multiplies by 10 to give
352 410, subtracts 35 241 to give 317 169, and adds 234 to give
317 403. Suppose you are then given the digits 3, 1, 4, 0 and 3,
(leaving out 7). Their sum is 11, and the nearest multiple of 9
above 11 is 18. Then 18 − 11 = 7 gives the missing digit.

Why does it work?

89 Optimising transport costs

EASIDRIVE, a national car hire firm, finds itself with an excess of cars at centres A, B and C, and a shortage of cars at centres P, Q, R and S. The excesses and shortages are as follows:

A: 9 cars   B: 6 cars   C: 8 cars
P: 5 cars   Q: 7 cars   R: 3 cars   S: 8 cars

Now there are many ways of redistributing the cars to redress the balance, and one such way is given in the first table. It shows for example, that 3 cars are moved from A to P, 2 from A to R and 4 from A to S.

Now this table was compiled without taking any account of the costs. However, the second table gives the cost, in tens of pounds, of moving individual cars between the centres, so by using it we can see the cost of the above redistribution:

3 × £60 + 2 × £50 + 4 × £40 + £40 + 4 × £50
    + £80 + £30 + 3 × £40 + £70 + 3 × £50
= £1130

Now the viability of the firm depends on it always making these redistributions as cheaply as possible.

How should the cars be moved to minimise the cost?

car movements

to

		P	Q	R	S	
	A	3	0	2	4	9
from	B	1	4	0	1	6
	C	1	3	1	3	8
		5	7	3	8	

distribution costs

to

		P	Q	R	S
	A	6	2	5	4
from	B	4	5	3	8
	C	3	4	7	5

90 Pentagonal magic!

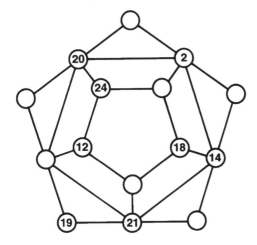

Allocate a different number to each of the fifteen points in the figure shown so that the five numbers at the vertices of each of the eight pentagons total 65.

Is it possible to allocate the numbers 1 to 15 to the points to make the eight pentagons magic in the same way?

91 Squaring up with 1 to 9

There are 30 different square numbers containing each of the digits 1 to 9 only once. Here, for example, are 2 of them:

$$215\,384\,976 = 14\,676^2$$
$$\text{and}\quad 743\,816\,529 = 27\,273^2$$

This seems surprising, until you realise that there are $9 \times 8 \times 7 \times 6 \times 5 \times 4 \times 3 \times 2 \times 1 = 362\,880$ different permutations of the nine digits. Now if you want a real challenge you could try to find the other 28 square numbers! But be satisfied with solving these less daunting challenges. Find:

(a) five square numbers
(b) four square numbers
(c) three square numbers,

which in each case use up all the nine digits between them without repetition.

How many different solutions can you find for each?

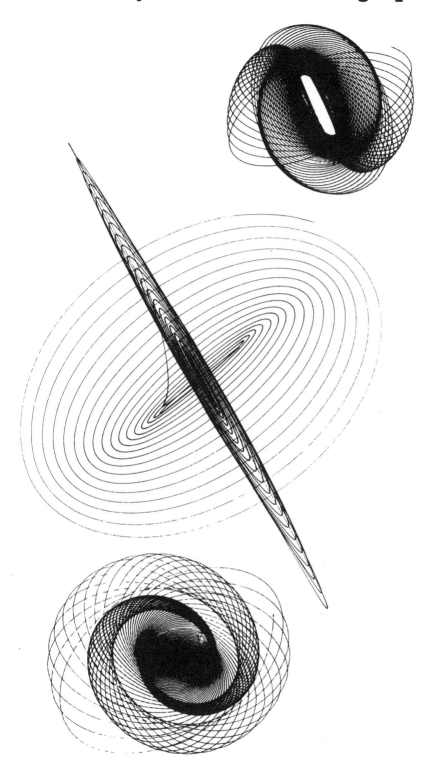

In many Victorian drawing rooms a machine could be found which produced patterns of the kind shown on page 50. These machines, known as harmonographs depended on the oscillating motion of a pendulum for their effect. They were usually made by skilled craftsmen out of metal, but this is not necessary. Very effective harmonographs can be made, quite simply, by building on a larger scale: three approaches are described here. The author made the first to be described in half an hour, from materials found in the garden shed!

The paving slab harmonograph

The weight used in the first harmonograph was a paving slab, as used by countless gardeners everywhere. It was suspended by two loops of clothes-line from the hooks of a swing frame, as shown, so that it could swing close to the ground. (Two hooks in any handy beam or lintel would do as well, or in the branch of a suitable tree.) The paving slab, being flat, was used for the table of the harmonograph, and to make a smoother surface for the paper a piece of hardboard was placed over it. The paving slab was free to oscillate as a conical pendulum, that is round and round like a conker on a string not simply to and fro like the pendulum of a clock. It is this motion that is responsible for the attractive patterns produced.

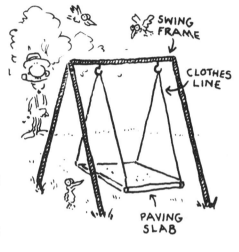

All that remained was to fix a ball-point pen in such a way that it stayed in contact with the table, with sufficient pressure for it to draw, as the paving slab swung around in ever decreasing oscillations. This was achieved by taking a strip of wood about a metre long and screwing it to a second piece about 30 cm long, at right angles to it at its point of balance, to form a cross (see the diagram).

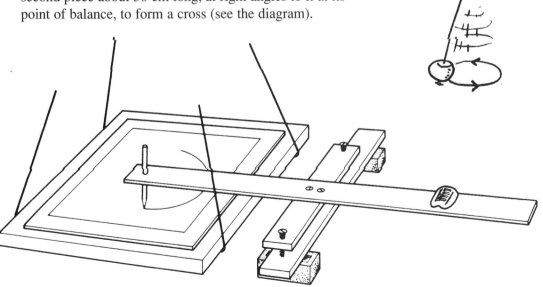

A wood screw was then screwed through each end of the cross-piece so that it protruded about 1 cm through the wood to act as a pivot. This pen-arm was then pivoted on a suitably placed piece of wood so that it could see-saw with one end over the centre of the paving slab. A hole was drilled through the end of the arm just large enough to take a ball-point pen, and the pressure of the pen on the paper was adjusted by moving a small stone along the arm as a counterbalance. (NB the cross-piece is necessary to prevent sideways movement of the pen-arm.)

To operate the harmonograph a sheet of paper was placed on the hardboard, centred under the pen, and held in place by some smaller stones from the flower bed. With the pen-arm tilted so that the pen was not in contact with the paper the paving slab was set in motion. The pen was then tilted to make contact with the paper and the swinging slab did the rest. When the design being traced out had reached a satisfactory point the arm was tilted to raise the pen from the paper.

Different designs can be superimposed on top of one another in the same or different colours to create an endless number of patterns. However, with this simple harmonograph the designs will all be based on versions of elliptical spirals.

The broom handle harmonograph

The basis of this harmonograph consists of two broom handles suitably pivoted, and weighted, to form pendulums as shown in the diagram. It was originally made for the author in this way by a group of 12-year-old boys who operated it very successfully. However, it would probably be even more effective if the broom handles were replaced by wooden dowelling with much smaller cross-section, as obtainable in most DIY stores.

The two pendulums swing at right angles to one another. The right-hand pendulum swings from front to back and carries the table to which the paper is fixed. The left-hand pendulum, on the other hand, swings from left to right and carries the pen-arm. This is in contrast to the paving slab harmonograph where the pen is essentially fixed. Furthermore, by varying the heights of the weights on the pendulums their time of swing can be changed relative to one another and this enables more intricate patterns to be produced.

In constructing a harmonograph of this kind try to keep all the moving parts, other than the weights, as light as possible consistent with being rigid. It is also important to have pivots which offer very little resistance to motion so that the pendulums take a long time to come to rest. The author has found that two nuts and a bolt, whose end has been filed to a chisel section and rests in the head of a conventional wood screw, make a very effective pivot which has the

Each pendulum should be pivoted so that about 25 cm is above the pivot and, say 75 cm below, but the best height can be found by experiment. The weights on the pendulums need to be as heavy as possible within reason. A heavy piece of metal with a hole through it would be fine, but weights can be made by filling tin cans with concrete. Make the weights with a hole right through them, then they can be slid up or down the rod of the pendulum and fixed at a suitable height by putting a nail through a hole already drilled in the rod.

A Meccano harmonograph

This harmonograph can be constructed by anyone with access to some Meccano. The Meccano parts are used to make a set of 'compass gimbals' to support the pendulum holding the table. The gimbals, see the diagram, allow the table pendulum to swing in any direction, so that the pen arm needs only to move freely in a vertical plane, as with the paving slab harmonograph. The gimbals do not have to be made exactly as shown, but the two gimbal rings need to be made as rigid as possible, yet free to rotate about perpendicular axes without any sideways movement.

A refill from a standard ball-point is an ideal light pen which can be incorporated in a light pen-arm. Consequently the whole harmonograph can be made very compactly and set up in a limited space.

If the pendulum can be pivoted well off the ground then a second conical pendulum can be suspended underneath the first by hanging a weight on a wire attached to a hook in its base. This added complexity leads to much more variety in the possible designs which can be traced, but careful experimenting will be required between the ratios of the weights, and the length of the pendulum, to achieve good results.

pen arm

table

compass gimbals

weight

93 Find that angle!

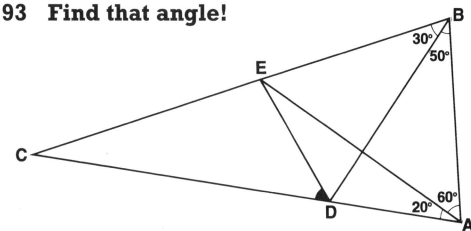

In the diagram, four angles are given and it is an easy matter to work out many of the other angles in the figure.

On the way you will find that the figure contains three isosceles triangles – so what is there left to find? Well the challenge is to find the size of angle *CDE*. Use whatever mathematical knowledge you have at your disposal, but only give yourself top marks if you solve it using Euclidean geometry.

94 Jigsaw conjectures

Mary Multipiece enjoyed making jigsaws, so she was delighted to find a new jigsaw among her many Christmas presents. It had 736 pieces and would make up into a rectangular picture 24 inches long by 17 inches high. Mary always started her jigsaws by finding all the edge pieces and fitting them together to frame the picture. Only then did she pay attention to the details of the rest of the picture. On this occasion she couldn't get started as the table was needed for a party, so she amused herself by trying to decide how many edge pieces her new jigsaw contained before she even opened the box. She made her calculation and was delighted to find that, on opening the box and extracting all the edge pieces, she had in fact determined the exact number. Could you have done?

95 Wayward's new coinage system!

After a military coup, the new President-General of the Wayward Isles decided to indulge his fantasy for a new coinage system. He had the idea that by choosing the right denominations for the islands' coins, most, if not all, of the everyday commercial transactions where money changed hands would be able to take place with the payment of at most *three* coins.

Now the main unit of exchange was the Freak (Fk), and it was essential that his system allowed payments of consecutive whole number quantities of Freaks, 1Fk, 2Fk, 3Fk, ... Clearly there is no need to make coins of every value, for example, if coins were only made in 1Fk and 4Fk denominations then it would be possible to make any payment from 1Fk to 6Fk, although 7Fk would not be possible.

1   1+1   1+1+1   4   4+1   4+1+1

This might appear to be the best solution if only two different coins are produced, but in fact 1Fk and 3Fk coins would be better, giving possible payments of 1Fk to 7Fk:

1   1+1   1+1+1   3+1   3 +1+1   3+3   3+3+1

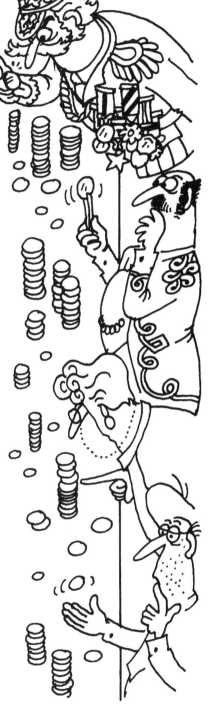

with 8Fk not being possible in less than 4 coins.

The President's advisors were no fools, and knew their future depended on finding a successful outcome for his fantasy. First they found that by the right selection of three values for their coins they could achieve any total from 1Fk to 15Fk. They then showed that with four different values they would be able to achieve all possible totals from 1Fk to 24Fk.

Which values were needed to satisfy these conditions?

If you had to advise the President – and your life depended on it – what value coins would you choose to produce to optimise the possible totals if you were allowed five different values?

96 Ibrahim's tile torment!

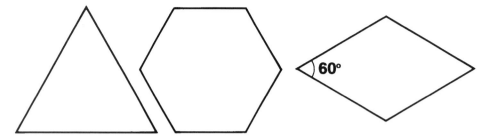

Tiles are made in three shapes by the Tessellation Tile Company: equilateral triangles, regular hexagons and diamonds. Owing to a peculiar quirk of the company's managing director, Sir Cumference, they all had perimeters of the same length.

Now Ibrahim had brought a house with a patio made from 288 of the company's triangular tiles. But they had been in place a long time and he wanted to replace them with either the hexagonal or the diamond-shaped tiles. He sat down with a piece of paper and a pencil to try to work out how many tiles he would need to buy if he chose hexagons, or if he chose diamonds. After a wastepaper basket full of his many false attempts he decided he had better take his problem to the Tessellation Tile Company.

Could you have helped him? You may assume there are no boundary problems.

97 How large are the circles?

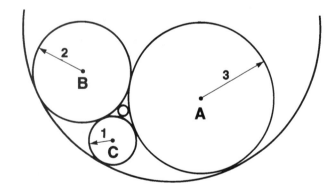

Three circles with centres A, B and C, and radii 3 cm, 2 cm and 1 cm are drawn to touch each other as shown. Two further circles are drawn to touch these three circles, one sitting in between them and the other enclosing them. The challenge is to find the radii of these two circles.

98 Packing perfume profitably

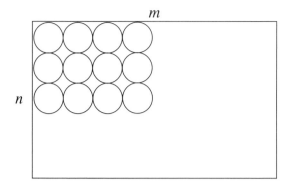

Bottles of expensive perfume are carefully packed by the manufacturer in specially-made rectangular boxes to hold one layer of the circular cross-section containers. There were n rows of m bottles in each box, tightly packed together. The duty on each bottle when imported to the UK was very high, so any bottle which could escape the scrutiny of the customs made a good profit for the importer.

Now Hex Agonal, the flamboyant importer, was not averse to pulling the wool over the customs' eyes and he could see that, although the bottles were tightly packed in their box, he could pack them differently and make room for just one more bottle. Recognising this fact, he bought enough boxes of the perfume so that the contents of one box could be put, one at a time, into the repacked remaining boxes. With luck, the customs officers would let them through without opening the boxes and he would have smuggled in the equivalent of a boxful of perfume without paying duty on it.

Work out the smallest box which could take an extra bottle of perfume, and hence the smallest number of boxes that Hex Agonal could have purchased.

99 Primeval magic!

Get a friend to take any prime number greater than 3, square it, add 32, then divide by 12 and record the remainder. You can now surprise your friend by telling them the remainder, which will always be 9. Alternatively, you could ask them to tell you the figures after the decimal point – these will always be 0.75. Why is this?

100 Golfing gymnastics!

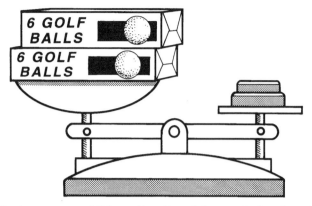

The inspectors of fair trading found that a wholesaler of golfing equipment was swindling his retailers by including one box of substandard golf balls to every nine boxes of top grade balls he sold them. Each box contained 6 golf balls, and the external appearance of all the balls was identical. However, the substandard balls were each 1 gram too light. The retailers were informed of this discrepancy. The boxes all arrived in packs of ten, each with one substandard box – but which one?

Sidney Sixiron, the professional at a prestigious golf course, had just taken delivery of a large order so needed to sort them out quickly. He soon found a way to do this which required only one weighing for each batch of ten boxes, using a pair of scales and a set of weights. How did he do it?

Note that he did not need to know what a golf ball should weigh.

101 A sixth-order difference triangle

Rearrange the 21 numbered balls into a triangular array as given, but each ball after the first row must be placed so that its number is equal to the difference of the numbers on the two balls immediately above which touch it.

Note the numbers given include all those from 1 to 22 but leaving out 15.

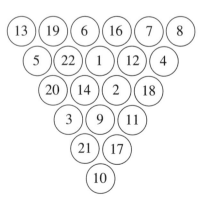

102 Grandfather's deliberations!

Professor Integer had spent a lifetime researching the properties of whole numbers, so even though he was now retired he didn't miss interesting coincidences relating to numbers. One day he realised that his son's age plus those of his four granddaughters equalled his own. What is more, his son's age and granddaughters' ages were all different Fibonacci numbers (1, 1, 2, 3, 5, 8, 13, …). As if that wasn't enough his own age corresponded to the smallest number which could not be expressed by the sum of fewer than five different Fibonacci numbers. So what were all their ages?

103 Triangulation?

The four fields represented by the adjoining maps are up for sale as a building site, and the surveyor has surveyed them and given the measurements shown. The local authority regulations require that the plot for each house is a minimum of 450 square metres. A builder looked at the surveyor's measurements and calculated the area of the site from the length of the base of the site as 160 m and its height as 130 m to be $\frac{1}{2} \times 160 \times 130 = 10400$ m. So by dividing by 450 he reckoned he would be able to build 23 houses on the site and based his bidding accordingly. However, when he sought planning permission at a later stage, the planning committee calculated the area of the site by working out the areas of each of the fields separately and concluded that the site had an area of 10 300 m, so only 22 houses could be built. Clearly, they cannot both be right! Sort it out!

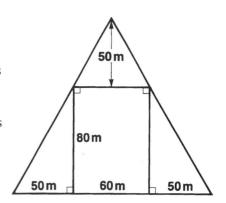

104 Circles into squares!

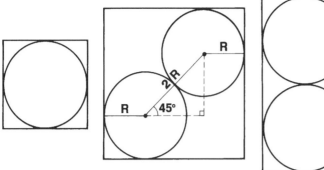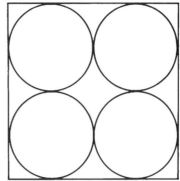

The challenge here is to find the dimensions of the smallest square into which you can pack a number of identical circles. Take, for example, some identical circular coins and see how best to arrange them to minimise the size of the square to contain them. With 1, 2 or 4 coins the solutions are easily seen as those shown above. If the radius of the coin is R, then the lengths of sides of the corresponding squares are

$$2R, \quad 2R + \sqrt{2}R \approx 3.414R \text{ and } 4R.$$

But it is not always so obvious to see which arrangements of coins to take. Below shows two ways of fitting a square around 3 coins. The first leads to a square of side $2R + 2\sqrt{2}R \approx 4.828R$, whilst the second has side $4R$. But these can be improved upon. What is the optimum solution?

Now test yourself by finding the smallest square to contain 5, 6, 7 and 8 coins.

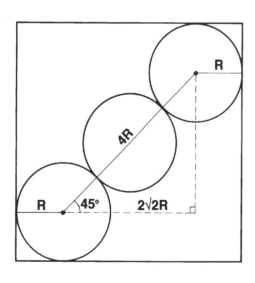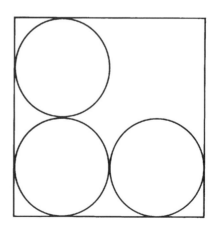

105　Minimising manpower!

A team of three explorers plan an expedition through an Amazonian rain forest to a distant settlement which it is estimated they can reach in 12 days of trekking. On reaching the settlement they will radio for a helicopter to pick them up and return them to their base. However, they plan to be self-supporting for the 12-day trek, relying on porters for all their needs. The explorers will carry the scientific research equipment between them, while the porters will carry all the other provisions for the explorers and themselves. Previous experience in the area shows that a porter can be expected to carry sufficient provisions for the equivalent of 10 person-days. It is not safe to leave caches of stores on the way, so everything required for the 12-day journey must be carried by the porters. The porters can either complete the journey or trek back to base without going the whole way. Decisions about which, if any, porters return to base are made at the beginning of each day. Now reliable porters are both difficult to recruit and expensive so the explorers want to use them as efficiently as possible.

What is the smallest number of porters the explorers can employ, assuming that all the provisions for the trek have to be carried from day one?

106 The chain challenge

Karen and Alan's teacher, Mr Khan set them to investigate chains of numbers formed by starting with any whole number, adding 1 if it was odd, and halving it when it was even, continuing in the same way until they ended in 1, as shown by the flow diagram.

As an example, he gave them:

$$13 \rightarrow 14 \rightarrow 7 \rightarrow 8 \rightarrow 4 \rightarrow 2 \rightarrow 1$$

which, starting with 13, reached 1 after 6 steps.

After a time Mr Khan challenged them to find which number less than 2000 would give the longest chain.

Alan immediately turned to the computer to help, programming it to test each number in turn, starting from 2000 and working down. But Karen, always a more reflective student, decided it wasn't such a daunting problem as it first appeared and soon had the correct answer.

How long will it take you?

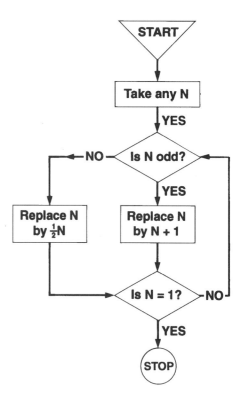

107 Reflections in their prime!

As they celebrated yet one more Christmas together sitting in front of an open log fire, Agnes, Emily and Mabel, three spinster sisters, reflected on the number of the year, 1997. After some thought they decided that this was a prime number. This had them considering their ages. Agnes, the eldest, and Mabel, the youngest, found that their ages were also prime numbers, but that Emily's was a square number. Now their ages differed by 2 years, so when were they born?

Thinking of earlier Christmases, they realised there was only one other when their ages had similar properties, and there was one celebrated Christmas when they were all of prime age. When did these events occur?

108   Every triangle is isosceles?

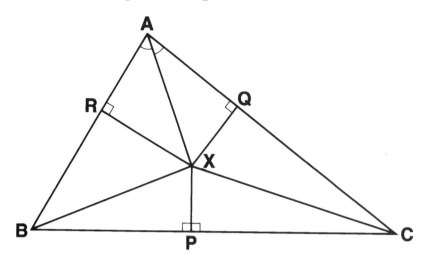

Starting with any triangle *ABC*, let the angle bisector of angle *A* meet the perpendicular bisector of side *BC* at *X*. From *X* draw the perpendiculars *XR* and XQ to *AB* and *AC* respectively. Then:

(i) So triangles *AXR* and *AXQ* are congruent.
  AX is common, to triangles *AXR* and *AXC*
  angle *RAX* = angle *QAX* from the construction
  angle *ARX* = angle *AQX* = 90º
  Hence *AR* = *AQ*

(ii) So triangles *BXR* and *CXQ* are congruent.
  BX = *CX*, as *PX* is the perpendicular bisector
  RX = *QX*, from the congruence of the previous triangles
  angle *BRX* = angle *CQX* = 90º
  Hence *RB* = *QC*
  So *AB* = *AR* + *RB* = *AQ* + *QC* = *AC*,
  thus proving that triangle *ABC* is isosceles!

Continuing with the same approach, we can prove *CA* = *CB*, and hence the triangle is equilateral!

Where is the flaw in the argument?

109   What comes next?

(a) 2   4   9   18   23   46   51   __   __
(b) 2   4   3   9   8   64   63   __   __
(c) 2   4   5   7   9   10   11   13   __   __

110 Pipe packing

The Ace Alloy Extrusion Company prided itself on the excellence of its products and sent them all over the world. One of its specialities was the manufacture of high specification pipes. These were sent out in crates, tailor-made for each order, so that the pipes lay side by side on a flat surface. Often the orders would be for a range of pipes of different diameters and the manager in charge of packing them always placed them side by side starting with the largest diameter and working down to the smallest. But one day a bright, young efficiency expert came along and showed him how he could often reduce the size of his crates. She illustrated it by taking six pipes of external radii 10 cm, 8 cm, 5 cm, 3 cm, 2 cm and 2 cm.

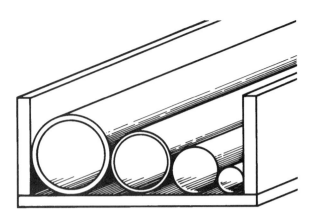

Find what internal width the crate would have required following the manager's normal plan, and the minimum width achievable by placing the pipes side by side in a different order.

111 Prof. Nilfactor's telephone number!

Professor Nilfactor, a world-renowned expert in the theory of numbers was ecstatic when he discovered the unique properties of his 8-digit telephone number. Not only was the number itself prime, but the 7-digit, 6-digit, 5-digit, 4-digit, 3-digit, 2-digit and single-digit numbers formed by successively removing the right-hand digit were also prime. He investigated all such numbers, and found many others with the same property such as 593 993 where

593 993   59 399   5939   593   59   and   5

are all prime. But he was delighted to find that his telephone number corresponded to the largest number with this property.

What was the professor's number?

112 Elliptical areas

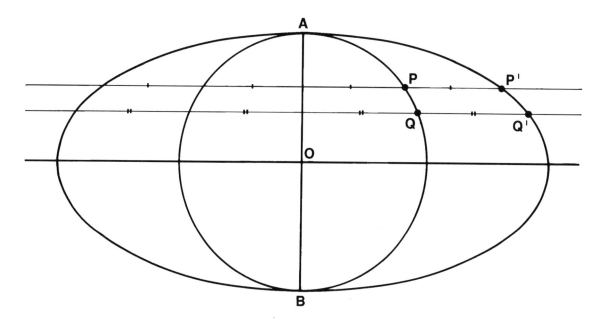

The ellipse is a very common shape, for it is the shape we see whenever we view a circular object, such as the top of a jam jar, from an angle. Many arches of bridges have an elliptical cross section, and the paths traced out by orbiting satellites are ellipses. The ellipse can be drawn in many ways, but one way described here helps us to see the relation of an ellipse to a circle, and how their areas are related.

Start by drawing a circle, see the diagram, and draw in its vertical diameter AOB. Now draw a series of parallel lines across the circle at right-angles to AOB. The circle is now stretched in the direction of the parallel lines by a scale factor of 2 as follows. Mark points like P' and Q' on the lines which are twice as far from AOB as P and Q, the points where the circle cuts the lines. When you have enough points, join them by a smooth curve to form an ellipse which is twice as long as it is high. Any other scale factor can be used to stretch the circle to form an ellipse with any proportions you like.

Now for the challenges. If the circle has a radius of R, what is the area of:

(a) the ellipse
(b) the largest quadrilateral you can draw with each of its vertices on the boundary of the ellipse?

113 Matrix voyages!

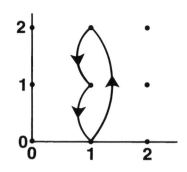

In the fantasy world of finite mathematics, a two-dimensional world exists with only 9 points (see the diagram), whose co-ordinates are $(0,0)$, $(1,0)$, $(2,0)$, $(0,1)$, $(1,1)$, $(2,1)$, $(0,2)$, $(1,2)$ and $(2,2)$. Starting at the point $(1,0)$, a traveller can travel to other points by using a matrix to transfer from one to another. All operations are performed in modulo 3 arithmetic. (Use ordinary arithmetic, divide the answer by 3 and only keep the remainder!)

For example, the matrix $\begin{pmatrix} 1 & 0 \\ 2 & 1 \end{pmatrix}$ takes the traveller from $(1,0)$

to $(1,2)$ as $\begin{pmatrix} 1 & 0 \\ 2 & 1 \end{pmatrix} \begin{pmatrix} 1 \\ 0 \end{pmatrix} = \begin{pmatrix} 1 \\ 2 \end{pmatrix}$

The next port of call will be $(1,1)$ as $\begin{pmatrix} 1 & 0 \\ 2 & 1 \end{pmatrix} \begin{pmatrix} 1 \\ 2 \end{pmatrix} = \begin{pmatrix} 1 \\ 1 \end{pmatrix}$, but

then the traveller will be returned to $(1,0)$ as $\begin{pmatrix} 1 & 0 \\ 2 & 1 \end{pmatrix} \begin{pmatrix} 1 \\ 1 \end{pmatrix} = \begin{pmatrix} 1 \\ 0 \end{pmatrix}$

This matrix gave a very limited view of the world, but

show that the matrix $\begin{pmatrix} 1 & 2 \\ 1 & 1 \end{pmatrix}$ will take the traveller step by step to every

point except $(0,0)$ before returning to the point $(1,0)$.

Now find other matrix manipulators to take you on a voyage around the world.

If you managed that, try finding matrix manipulators in the finite world consisting of the 25 points with coordinates from $(0, 0)$ to $(4, 4)$ which will take the traveller from $(1, 0)$ to all the 24 points other than the origin before returning to base. But this time you need to operate in modulo 5 arithmetic!

114 The surprising sphere

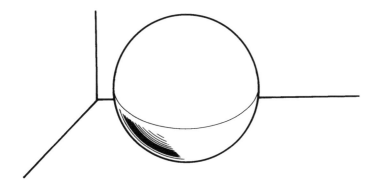

While setting questions for a mathematics exam, the mathematics teacher wanted to find some points on the surface of a sphere with integer coordinates. In the question he eventually set, he used the points:

$A(3,6,14)$ $B(11,2,6)$ $C(4,13,4)$ $D(1,10,10)$

In the process, however, he was astonished to realise that the sphere he had chosen contained *over 100 points on its surface whose coordinates were all positive integers!*

Can you find the radius and coordinates of the centre of this sphere, given that they are also integers, and find just how many points there are on its surface with integer coordinates?

COMMENTARY

1 Complete the cube

An identical solid to that given would make a $2 \times 2 \times 2$ cube.

2 Jasmine's friends

Jasmine had 12 friends and they had four apples and one orange. This is because $299 = 23 \times 13$; 13 cannot be expressed as a number of 4s and a number of 7s, while 23 is equal to four 4s plus 7.

3 Building to order!

These are 16 possible solutions: the 8 shown together with their mirror images in the NW–SE diagonal.

```
1 5 3    1 8 3    1 7 3    1 8 3
8 2 6    7 2 5    8 2 5    4 2 6
4 7 9    4 6 9    6 4 9    7 5 9

1 3 6    1 4 7    1 5 7    1 6 4
4 8 2    5 8 2    4 8 2    5 8 2
7 5 9    3 6 9    6 3 9    7 3 9
```

4 Matchstick mansions

One match is all that is required for (a) or (b), but (c) will require five as shown.

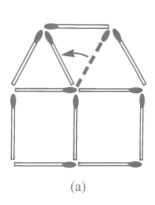

(a)

(b)

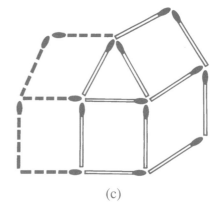

(c)

5 Make 24

Here are six solutions

$$22 + 2 = 24 \qquad\qquad 3^3 - 3 = 24$$
$$4! \times (4/4) = 24 \qquad 5!/\sqrt{(5 \times 5)} = 24$$
$$(\sqrt{9})! + 9 + 9 = 24 \qquad (\sqrt{9})^{\sqrt{9}} - \sqrt{9} = 24$$

There may be others and I would be happy to hear from you if you find any.

6 Symbolic interpretations!

IV PLUS IX PLUS V = EIGHTEEN

V PLUS V $\qquad\quad$ = TEN

7 Sort out the symbols!

Both missing totals are 30.

It is tempting to solve this puzzle by trial and error using whole numbers, but each of the symbols is in fact a number ending in a quarter.

$\blacklozenge$ = 6.25 $\quad\bullet$ = 8.25 $\quad\blacktriangle$ = 9.25 $\quad\blacksquare$ = 7.25

To solve the problem, let

$\blacklozenge$ = a $\quad\bullet$ = b $\quad\blacktriangle$ = c $\quad\blacksquare$ = d

From the first and third rows and the third and fourth columns we get:

$$a + 2b + c \qquad\quad = 32 \quad \text{①}$$
$$a + 2b \qquad + d = 30 \quad \text{②}$$
$$2a \qquad + 2c \qquad = 31 \quad \text{③}$$
$$\quad 2b \qquad + 2d = 31 \quad \text{④}$$

From equation ③, we get $a + c = 15.5$.
Substituting this in the first equation gives $b = 8.25$.
Putting this value for b equation ④ gives $d = 7.25$.
Substituting these values for b and d in equation ② gives $a = 6.25$.
Finally, putting this value of a into equation ③ gives $c = 9.25$.

8 Journeying to St Ives

1 person, the reciter of the rhyme, was going to St Ives.

1 man, 7 wives, 49 sacks, 343 cats, 2401 kits, which equals 2801, were going **away** from St Ives!

9 Punishing perambulations!

The visitor has the alternative of 2 ways from *A* to *B*, 2 ways from *B* to *C*, 2 ways from *C* to *D*, 9 ways from *D* to *E* (3 direct and 6 via *XY*), and finally 2 ways from *E* to *A*.

So there are $2 \times 2 \times 2 \times 9 \times 2 = $ **144 different ways** around the garden!

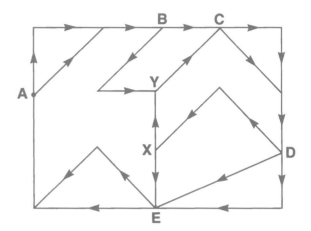

To see all the exhibits a visitor will need to make a minimum of **4 circuits**, because there are 3 direct ways from *D* to *E* as well as the need to make at least 1 journey along *XY*.

Now for the tricky question: how many different ways could a visitor make 4 circuits and see all the exhibits?

10 Sale bargains?

Well, you would have saved on the original price.

Suppose the original price of a suite had been £1000, then its inflated price would have been £1200. 20% off £1200 is £240 less than £1200, that is £960, so you would have saved £40 on the original price. So the '20% off the marked price!' represents a 4% saving on the original price.

Not such a good bargain!

11 Three in a line

David's original array has 6 sets of counters lying three to a line. They are indicated by the solid lines. There is just one position as shown where a counter can be placed to add four more lines. There are also three other positions to be found where a counter would add three new lines.

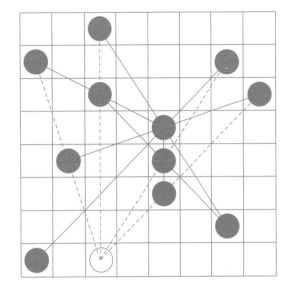

12 Age related

Katherine: 34
Rosemary: 43
Father: 68
Grandmother: 86

There are fourteen sets of numbers satisfying

$$ab \times cd = ba \times dc$$

where the digits are not repeated and of these, only the above satisfies the additional constraints of the puzzle.

See also activity 24.

13 Cross out!

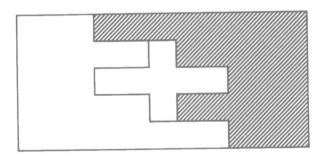

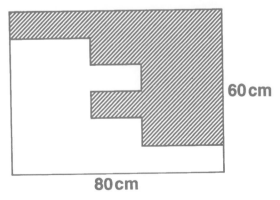

60 cm

80 cm

14 What scores are possible?

Not everyone is familiar with the triangle numbers. They are those numbers which can be expressed in the form
$1 + 2 + 3 + \ldots + n$,
for example $6 = 1 + 2 + 3$ and $21 = 1 + 2 + 3 + 4 + 5 + 6$.

The only two-digit ones are:
01 03 06 10 15 21 28 36 45 55 66 78 91

Remember that 01 is not a prime number although it is both a triangle number and a square number.

The highest score is 23 and can be achieved in many ways.

The following are optimum solutions gleaned from various sources including friends in Brunei and Japan to whom I have introduced the puzzle:

8973641025	8971025364
8364102597	8364710259
0253641978	0253641789

Note in each case the use of 02, the only two-digit number ending in 2 which is prime, and of 36, the only two-digit number which is both square and triangular.

An example of a sequence which has a zero score is:

9085127634

It is my hunch that all scores between 0 and 23 are also possible, but you can prove me wrong!

15 Triangular trios

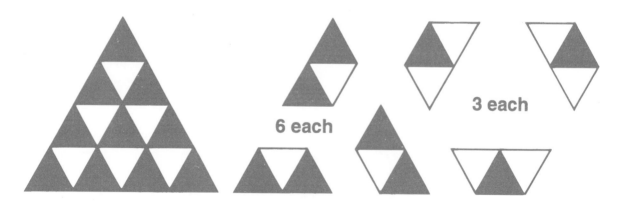

6 each

3 each

27 ways in all. They are to be found as indicated in the above diagram.

16 Cubical configurations

The nets all fold to make cubes, but only the third one could make the dice shown, assuming that the orientation of the digits 3, 5, and 6 is correct. In the first net the 3 is on the opposite face to the 6 so cannot be correct. The second net has all the numbers on the correct faces but the 1 would need to be upside-down, not on its side, to have the correct orientation with respect to the 4 and the 2.

17 Crosswords

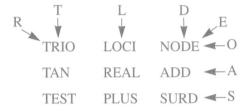

This solution is unique apart from reflections and rotations. This puzzle can be solved systematically by finding sets of three words with common letters and ensuring that you do not use any other word which contains that common letter. The word in the centre must belong to four sets, the words in the corners to three sets, and the words in the middle of the sides to two sets. The word ISOSCELES was put in to confuse the situation, for it contains many of the common letters; if you try to include it in your array you will have four words with a common letter, which then does not satisfy the given criteria.

I attempted to make up this puzzle using longer mathematical words, but after many aborted attempts had to be satisfied with the above. Can you do better?

18 Counter change!

The game is described in *Creative Puzzles of the World* By Delft and Botermans (Cassell Ltd), under the name 'Switch Sixteen', where a solution is given in 52 moves. A very attractive boxed version of the game called Enigma, with coloured pegs in a wooden base, is produced by The Lagoon Trading Company of Kingston upon Thames but naturally no solution is given. I found a solution with 50 moves, which pleased me until my friend Yoshio Kimura from Kobe University of Commerce, Japan, sent me this very efficient solution needing only 46 moves.

Each intersection of the grid has been labelled by a letter, and a move is then uniquely given by indicating the position of the counter being moved. Moves which involve jumping over a counter of the opposite colour have been asterisked. This solution has a very satisfying symmetrical arrangement of the counters at the halfway stage as shown below.

h j* i f l* o i* g* d f* l* m j k i* c* b h* j* p* q o* i* g* a* b h* j* p* o i* c* f l* n* k i* g* h e f l* i h j* i

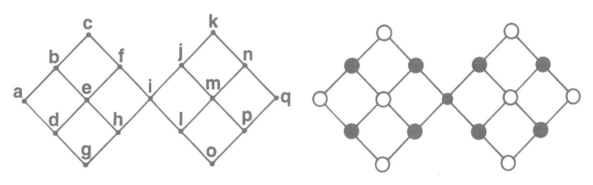

position after 23 moves

But is this the optimum solution?

19 All things being equal

All the computations in the array come to 8 if the arithmetical symbols are put in the order:

1st row ÷, ×, 2nd row +, −.

20 Safe cracking

A solution is found more easily when it is appreciated that the required condition is fulfilled if 8 switches are left unpressed in a pattern with an odd number in each row and column. There are many solutions, one of which is shown.

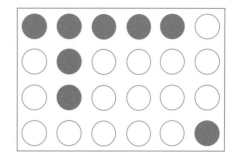

21 Donald's success?

   3 m × 1.5 m   3.5 m × 1.4 m   5 m × 1.25 m

It is not recorded whether the teacher checked to see how many other children in her class had added the length to the breadth to find the 'correct' answer!

In general, if $a = \dfrac{b}{(b-1)}$ then $a + b = ab$, so it is easy to generate pairs of numbers whose sum is equal to their product.

22 Manufacturing squares!

The wording of the puzzle is important. The first two parts do not say the squares have to be identical.

   The last part is achieved by making a cube, and this requires the movement of 8 matches.

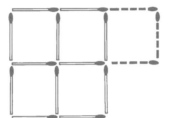 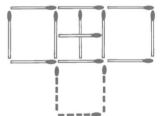

23 Motorway machinations!

Jane was 44 and she was born in 1936, so it was 1980 when she had these thoughts! The ten square numbers are:

   1 9 16 36 169 196 361 961 1369 1936

   $1849 = 43^2$ is the last year before 1936 which is a square number, so it would have been 1892 that someone might have made the same connections as Jane.

24 Turn about!

Clearly, if the two-digit numbers are both formed from repeated digits such as 22 and 55 then reversing the order of their digits leaves the numbers unchanged so their product will be the same. Also, if the second number is formed by reversing the digits of the first number, for example 12 and 21, then the same two numbers will be obtained by reversing the digits.

Suppose the two numbers are ab and cd, then we want their product to be equal to the product of ba and dc. This can be expressed algebraically as:

$$(10a + b)(10c + d) = (10b + a)(10d + c)$$

from which:

$$100ac + 10ad + 10bc + bd = 100bd + 10bc = 10ad + ac$$

giving: $$99ac = 99bd$$

So the numbers satisfy the required condition when their digits satisfy: $$ac = bd$$

This is equivalent to the product of the tens digits being equal to the product of the unit digits, giving the following solutions:

$12 \times 42 = 21 \times 24$	$24 \times 63 = 42 \times 36$
$12 \times 63 = 21 \times 36$	$24 \times 84 = 42 \times 48$
$13 \times 62 = 31 \times 26$	$23 \times 96 = 32 \times 69$
$12 \times 84 = 21 \times 48$	$26 \times 93 = 62 \times 39$
$14 \times 82 = 41 \times 28$	$34 \times 86 = 43 \times 68$
$13 \times 93 = 31 \times 39$	$36 \times 84 = 63 \times 48$
$23 \times 64 = 33 \times 46$	$46 \times 96 = 64 \times 69$

Far more solutions than at first seemed likely!

25 The open prison!

With 4 prisoners missing the remaining 20 prisoners had to distribute themselves 9 to a wall. There are surprisingly many solutions apart from rotations and reflections:

```
4 1 4   5 1 3   6 1 2   7 1 1   8 1 0
1   1   1   1   1   1   1   1   1   1
4 1 4   3 1 5   2 1 6   1 1 7   0 1 8

6 2 1   7 2 0   1 0 8   2 0 7   3 0 6
2   0   2   0   1   1   1   1   0   2
1 0 8   0 0 9   7 2 0   6 2 1   6 2 1
```

```
2 1 6    3 0 6    4 0 5    4 0 5    4 0 5
2   0    2   0    0   2    1   1    2   0
5 1 3    4 2 3    5 2 2    4 2 3    3 2 4
```

With the 4 missing prisoners returning with 4 friends there were 28 prisoners to distribute; there are at least 29 solutions, 10 of which are here.

```
0 5 4    1 5 3    2 5 2    6 2 1    7 2 0
5   5    5   5    5   5    2   8    2   8
4 5 0    3 5 1    2 5 2    1 8 0    0 8 1

8 1 0    2 4 3    1 5 3    1 3 5    0 4 5
1   9    7   0    6   4    8   2    7   3
0 9 0    0 6 3    2 5 2    0 7 2    2 6 1
```

26 Ayesha's offcuts

(i)   (ii)   (iii)

There are over 30 distinct solutions! The first one shown is one without a fault line. I think it is unique, but you may prove me wrong! Interchanging A and B gives the second solution in figure (ii). Interchanging B with D, interchanging A with E, and interchanging (A + E) with C leads to 9 solutions in all. Then this number of solutions is doubled by interchanging E with C. The effect of this on the first solution is given in figure (iii). It is now possible to permute E with A and B and also to interchange F with C to give many more solutions. No doubt there are even more solutions but these give you some idea of the potential!

27 A triple prime!

735

28 Coin magic!

There are only two solutions. He could have used three
1p coins, three 2p coins, three 5p coins and three 10p
coins to form the square shown with a magic total of 18.
The alternative solution multiplies the value of each
coin by 10, and so uses three 10p coins, three 20p
coins, three 50p coins and three 100p coins.

29 Mustafa's mosaics

Here are 21 solutions for 4×4, 5×5 and 6×6 patterns.
They are not exhaustive, and many 7×7 patterns are
possible using three 3×3 tiles, four 2×2 tiles and six 1×1
tiles.

Are there any solutions for 8×8 and 9×9 squares?

30 Lord Fearful's fortifications

There were 300 guards altogether, distributed as shown.

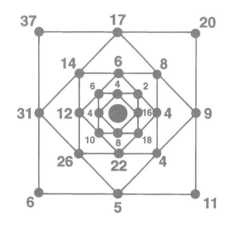

How did you solve this? Trial and error? A systematic search with a computer? There is a method of generating such sequences, starting with the smallest square, which I gleaned from Nigel Graves, a London school teacher.

Select the numbers for the small square, a, b, c, and d, such that:

$a \leq b \leq c$ and $d = a + b + c$

Then form A, B, C, and D using:

$A = \frac{1}{2}(c-a)$, $B = a+A$, $C = b+B$, $D = c+C$

A lies between d and a.

If $(c-a)$ is odd, double all the numbers before continuing.

31 Norman's radio aerial

A selection of possible routes, including the longest in each category, are shown below with their lengths to the nearest metre.

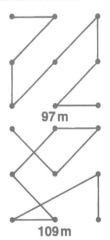

97 m

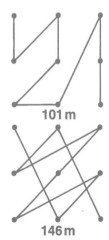

101 m

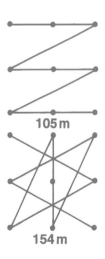

105 m

109 m

146 m

154 m

32 The three dice trick

The dots on the original top face and bottom face will always total 7, and all other faces contributing to the final total are now uppermost. So you only need to add together the dots on the top faces of the dice as they finish up and add 7.

33 The scouts' initiative test!

They overlapped the three planks as shown in the diagram.
You can convince yourself of the effectiveness of this
solution by using three rulers and three bottles or cans.

34 The rugger tournament

The total of the 'points for', 116, is equivalent to all the
points scored in the 3 matches, and also equal to the total of
'points against'. It follows that A has $116-38-49=29$ points
against them. Now the number of points scored in A's 2
matches is $39+29=68$, so the number of points in the match
between B and C is $116-68=48$. Similarly, the number of
points scored in A v. B and A v. C can be deduced as 25 and 43
respectively. Thus the drawn match must have been B v. C
and the score 24–24. So in their matches against A, B scored
11 and C scored 18. It follows that the match scores were:

A v. B 14–11   A v. C 25–18   B v. C 24–24

36 A cubical crawl

The spider has two alternative routes,
depending on which vertical face it
chooses. Imagine the top and the two
relevant sides flattened as in the diagram.
A shortest route will be one of the
straight lines from A to B across one of
the original vertical faces and the top.
If d is the length of an edge of the cube,
then using Pythagoras' theorem gives the
length of AB as $d\sqrt{5}$. But the spider takes
1 minute to crawl along an edge, so it will
take $\sqrt{5}$ minutes to crawl from A to B.

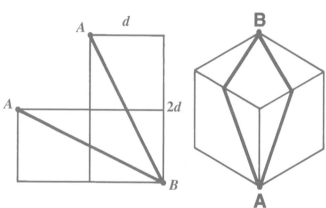

37 Only 'takes' and 'adds'

All totals are possible. Solutions are not unique. Simple
devices like changing '$+4-5$' to '$-4+5$' increase an existing
total by 2 and facilitate runs of totals once two adjacent totals
have been found.

38 Striking the hour

7.5 seconds. It takes 1.5 seconds between each strike.

39 A frog he would a-wooing go!

These are 2 possible routes through three areas of the garden and 1 possible route through the fourth, giving a total of 8 routes (other than going in the opposite direction. The diagrams show the 2 possible routes for each area.

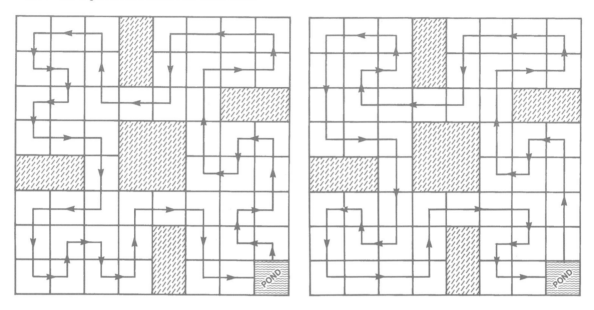

40 A fishy connection!

The idea for this puzzle came from a Japanese student. Note how the connection between the two shapes can best be understood in the overlapping tessellations shown.

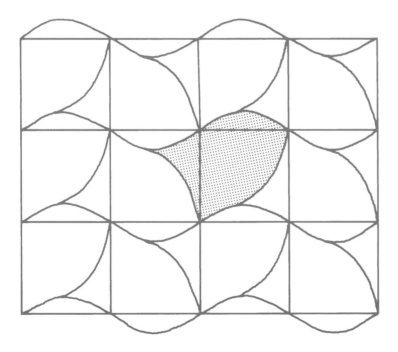

41 Pool-ball triangles

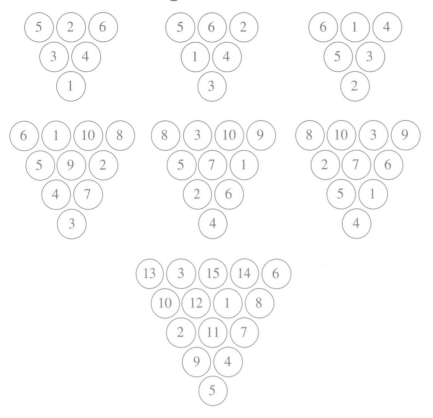

The solutions to (a) and (b), together with the only possible solution to the 15-ball problem, are given. It has been proved that no solution exists for larger triangles using consecutive numbers, but see puzzle 101. Anyone wanting to follow up these ideas might like to read the article by Charles W. Trigg. 'Absolute Difference Triangles' in *The Journal of Recreational Mathematics*, Vol.9(4), 1976–77, or Martin Gardner's book *From Penrose Tiles to Trapdoor Ciphers* (W. H. Freeman).

I met this problem originally in Japan where it was described as 'The bunch of grapes problem', so it has travelled well!

42 Magic squares to magic tetrahedra

The possible solutions are all based on the magic square shown here.

15	4	9	6
1	14	7	12
8	11	2	13
10	5	16	3

43 All ten digits!

Surprisingly there are two numbers with this property:
85 555 and 97 777.

$85\,555^2 - 1 = 7\,319\,658\,024$
$97\,777^2 - 1 = 9\,560\,341\,728$

44 By a whisker!

We may never know, but if the mouse takes the shortest path up the stairs it will just beat the cat to its home. Imagine the stairs made of folded card which can be flattened out into a rectangle as shown. Then the shortest route from A to B is the diagonal AB of length 172 cm to the nearest centimetre. So at 60 cm/s the mouse could get to its hole in just under 3 seconds and so beat the cat.

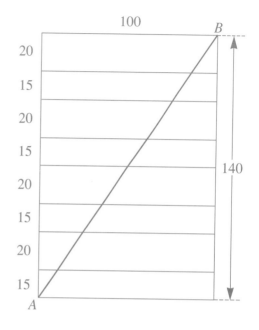

45 Pythagorean perimeters!

The key to solving this is to construct a list of Pythagorean triples and then to find the four smallest triangles with one side of the same length, to form the sides of the square.

These are (**12**, 16, 20), (9, **12**, 15), (5, **12**, 13) and (**12**, 35, 37), giving the ranch a perimeter of

$16 + 20 + 9 + 15 + 5 + 13 + 35 + 37 =$ **150 kilometres**.

(Note Pythagorean triples can be found from the formulae $m^2 - n^2$, $2mn$ and $m^2 + n^2$, where m and n are integers.)

46 Magic circles

One solution is shown. To solve this puzzle note that, for example, the circles on the right and left have no point in common so the magic total must be half the sum 1 to 8, i.e. 18. Note also how all the horizontal pairs sum to 9.

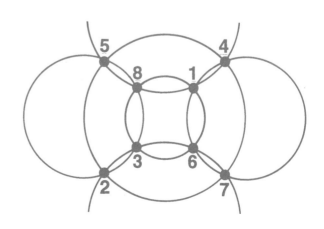

47 Armchair football

(a) There are $6 \times 4 = 24$ possible half-time scores.
In general, for a final score of m–n the number of possible half-time scores is $m \times n$.

(b) There are 56 ways in which the score could progress from 0–0 to 5–3. There are 8 goals scored, 5 by the home team and 3 by the away team, so the task is to see how many different sequences are possible using 5 Hs and 3 As. For example HHAHAAHH, HAHAHHAH. The number of ways is $8! / (5!\, 3!)$.
In general, for a final score of m-n the number of different scoring sequences is $(m + n)! / m!\, n!$

48 Commercialising Catch!

There are 126 cans, and there are only 5 cans in the top layer of the tallest wall.

This puzzle is based on expressing numbers as a sum of consecutive integers. All the counting numbers can be so expressed except powers of 2, such as 128 which is 2 raised to the power of 7. The representation of a given counting number as a sum of consecutive integers may be unique, for example $13 = 6 + 7$, but there may be many solutions as in this puzzle, where:

$$126 = 41 + 42 + 43$$
$$= 30 + 31 + 32 + 33$$
$$= 15 + 16 + 17 + 18 + 19 + 20 + 21$$
$$= 10 + 11 + 12 + 13 + 14 + 15 + 16 + 17 + 18$$
$$= 5 + 6 + 7 + 8 + 9 + 10 + 11 + 12 + 13 + 14 + 15 + 16$$

These solutions may be found by trial and error using a calculator.

49 Squaring squares!

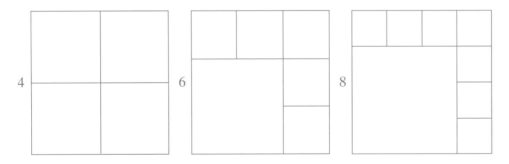

Consider the three solutions shown containing 4, 6 and 8 squares respectively. Any squares in the subdivision of each of these can be quartered into 4 squares so increasing the number in each by 3, giving 7, 9 and 11 squares respectively.

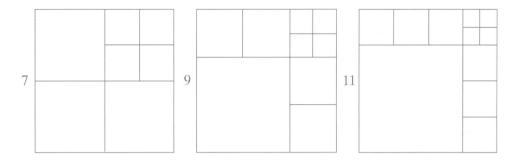

Further similar subdivisions of squares can increase the number of squares in steps of 3, and this process can continue *ad infinitum*, so solutions can be found for all $N \geq 6$. The only impossible subdivisions are for $N = 2, 3$ and 5.

Now try helping Sheik Mustafa in puzzle 29.

50 Seasonal visiting

Raheem's strategy takes him to his relatives in the order *ABCGFHJIDEA* with a total distance of 71 km. His route from *I* to *D* is via *J*, *H* and *F* of length 20 km, and his route from *D* to *E* is via *A*.

The shortest route he could have taken is *ABCGIJHFDAEA* of length 65 km. This solution was suggested by Margaret Walsh, a teacher at Ivybridge Community College.

51 Lunar areas

The lunar areas are equal to the area of the triangle. It is not as difficult to prove as may first appear. The figure can be thought of as having five regions. Let their areas be P, Q, R, S, and T as indicated on the diagram.

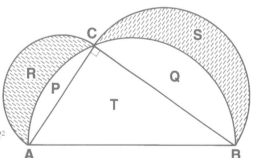

Then $R + P = \frac{1}{8}\pi AC^2$, $Q + S = \frac{1}{8}\pi BC^2$, $P + T + Q = \frac{1}{8}\pi AB^2$
But, by pythagoras' theorem, $AB^2 = AC^2 + BC^2$
So $P + T + Q = (R + P) + (Q + S)$ giving $T = R + S$

52 Cable connections

The minimum length of trench needed to be dug is 31 km. The Adjoining diagram shows which towns need to be connected directly. It is found by starting at any of these towns and then joining in the nearest town to the trench already cut at each stage. You may find it helpful to draw a network corresponding to all the roads to start with.

The exchange would be best built $\frac{1}{2}$ km along the road from D towards C, when A and F will then both be $12\frac{1}{2}$ km from it.

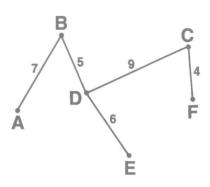

53 A matter of relative speed!

No, the answer is not 20 minutes!
They would take just 15 minutes.
Let Jenny and Jonathan's rowing speed be u
       the speed of the current be v
       the distance to be rowed be d.

Then $\dfrac{d}{(u+v)} = 10$ and $\dfrac{d}{(u-v)} = 30$

     giving $d = 10u + 10v$ and $d = 30u - 30v$

eliminating v gives $4d = 60u$,

from which $\dfrac{d}{u} = 15$

Regardless of the state of the tide, if they set out to row towards each other at the same time, they will approach each other at a speed of $2u$ and have a distance d to cover between them. Hence they will meet after $\dfrac{d}{2u} = 7\frac{1}{2}$ minutes.

54 Party politics!

The boys were paired off with the girls as follows:
    Akram with Yasmin, Chris with Anna, Eric with Karen, Martin with Emma, and Roger with Zoe. This gives the highest total of 'feel good' factors as 40.

    Roger has his first choice, while Ali, Chris and Eric have their second choice. Martin comes worst off with Emma, his third choice, but it was probably as well from her point of view as Martin had rated her significantly higher than any of the other boys.

55 Bridge building?

$AD + DC + CB = AB$, so D and C lie on top of AB! It follows that $DM = CM = 40$ cm.

56 Formation flying

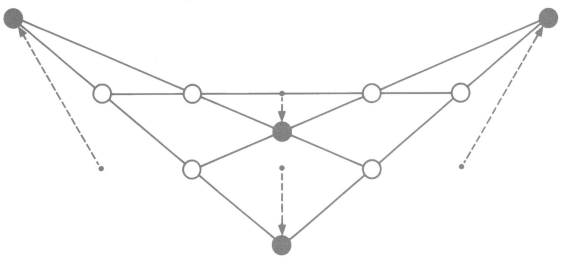

The diagram shows the new formation, with the blocked-in circles corresponding to the planes that moved. This puzzle could be treated as a coin puzzle. The trick in solving it is to consider ways in which five lines can intersect each other.

But a real clue is in the name of the formation team!

57 The robotic mouse!

First you must deduce the nature of the program. There are two aspects to this:

(i)   a right turn is followed by 2 left turns, by 3 right turns, by 4 left turns and so on;

(ii) the length of the leg following a right turn is half the previous leg, the length of leg following a left turn is double the previous leg. At the end of the 20th leg there are 2 more left turns before the next right turn, and at this point the mouse is 4.75 metres east and 5.5 metres south of its starting point.

58 Finding the centre

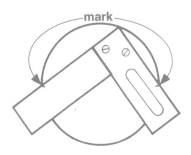

He puts the corner of the set square at the edge of a wheel and marks the edge of the wheel where the sides of the set square cross it (see the diagram). These points are at the ends of a diameter of the disc, so the carpenter now draws in the diameter using one edge of the set square. He turns the wheel around and constructs another diameter in the same way. Where the two diameters cross gives the centre.

59 Number wheels!

Solutions exist for totals from 22 to 38, except 30. The solution to the one started in the puzzle, which has a common total of 22, is given here, together with solutions for totals of 23, 24 and 26. Using the transformation $n \to 20-n$ transforms these into solutions with totals of 38, 37, 36 and 34. In searching for solutions it may help you to concentrate on fixing the nine even numbers first.

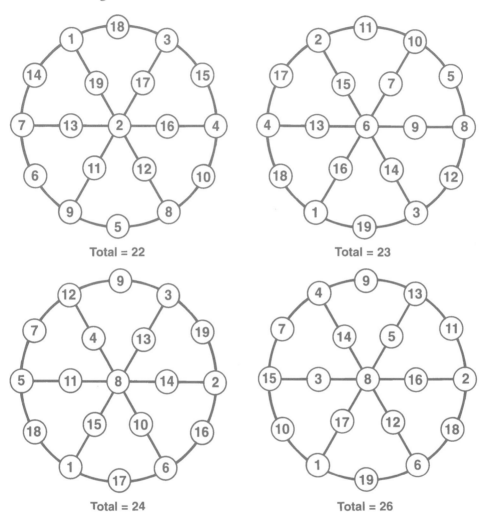

Total = 22

Total = 23

Total = 24

Total = 26

60 Equal products!

Here are three more solutions:

$$158 \times 32 = 5056 = 79 \times 64$$
$$584 \times 12 = 7008 = 96 \times 73$$
$$532 \times 14 = 7448 = 98 \times 76$$

The first is due to H. E. Dudeney, while the others were contributed by students of Professor Kimura, from Kobe, Japan

62 Where is the shopping centre?

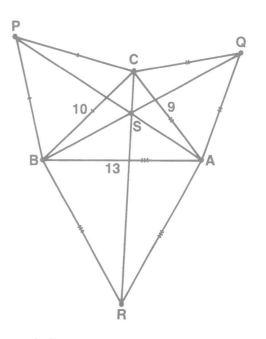

The optimum solution is found when the angles *ASB*, *BSC*, and *CSA* are all equal to 120°.

A neat construction for finding this point was given by J. E. Hoffman in 1929. He showed that if equilateral triangles *BPC*, *CQA* and *ARB* are drawn on the outside of triangle *ABC*, then *AP*, *BQ* and *CR* all intersect at the optimum point *S*. What is more, *AP*, *BQ* and *CR* are all equal in length and equal to $AS + BS + CS$. In this case:
$AS \approx 7.0$ km, $BS \approx 8$ km, $CS \approx 3.2$ km

63 Negotiating the corridor

The most likely shape for the table would have been a circle of radius 1 metre and area π square metres, (see the diagram).

There are shapes with larger areas which could negotiate the bend, but these are unlikely as tops of antique dining tables!

64 Marti's many routes!

208 days, corresponding to 208 different routes. This puzzle is based on one set by that master puzzler H. E. Dudeney almost 100 years ago. In considering the possible alternative routes, only the section from *B* to *E* need be considered, and all routes between them using 2, 3, 4, 5, or 6 stages.

		ways			ways
2 stages:	*BCE*	3	5 stages:	*BCDEDE*	18
	BDE	3		*BCBCDE*	18
				BDCEDE	6
3 stages:	*BCDE*	9		*BCDBCE*	6
	BDCE	1		*BDECDE*	6
				BDCBCE	6
4 stages:	*BCEDE*	18		*BDEDCE*	6
	BCBDE	18		*BCBDCE*	6
	BCBCE	6			
	BDEDE	6	6 stages:	*BCBCEDE*	36
				BCBDEDE	36

If you are brave, you might now like to consider all the 7 stage routes between *B* and *E*!

65 Fancy that!

3 785 942 160   4 753 869 120   4 876 391 520
are three further numbers with the same property.

66 Which route to follow?

There are three solutions:

$12 + 3 \times 2 - 6 \div 3 \times 4 - 2 \div 6 + 7 \div 3 = 4$
$12 + 3 \div 5 \times 6 \div 2 - 4 + 7 \div 3 = 4$
$12 + 3 \div 5 \times 7 - 9 + 6 \div 2 - 4 + 7 \div 3 = 4$

67 Triangular number tiles

Interchanging any or all of the pairs (7,5), (8,6) and (9,4) in the given solution will give another arrangement where the corner triangle numbers total 17. But other arrangements exist whose total is 17 which cannot be achieved in this way and one of them is given below. Also given below are solutions where the totals are 20 and 23.

The transformation $n \rightarrow 10 - n$ will always change a given solution into another solution. Solutions with a total of 17 map onto solutions with a total of 23 and vice versa. Solutions with a total of 20 map onto new solutions with a total of 20.

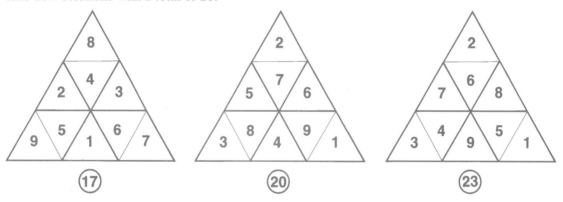

68 Panoramic possibilities!

I would never live long enough to see them all, for there are more than 6.2×10^{23} possible panoramic pictures, and at a second a time these would take approximately 2×10^{16} years

= 20 000 000 000 000 000 years.

In creating a picture there are 24 choices for the first card, 23 choices for the second card, 22 choices for the third card and so on, giving:

$24 \times 23 \times 22 \times 21 \times 20 \times \ldots \times 6 \times 5 \times 4 \times 3 \times 2 \times 1 = 24!$ choices in all.

69 Prime magic!

This square was first brought to my attention by Chris Meek, at Torquay Boy's G.S., who used his computer to take up my challenge of finding a 3×3 magic square with prime number entries. Knowing that the magic total is 15, it can be deduced that the number in the centre is 5, so for the four lines of three numbers through the centre the other numbers must sum to 10.

17	−13	41
29	5	−19
−31	53	−7

70 Traffic management

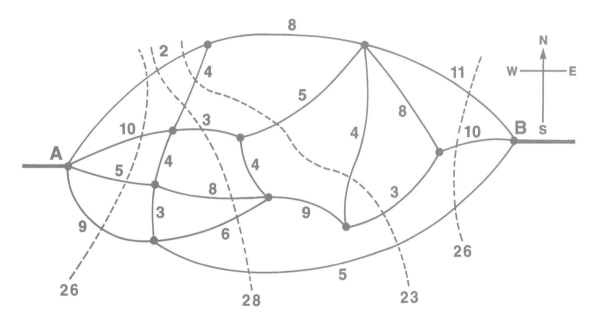

Although the roads leaving *A* and the roads approaching *B* each have a total capacity of 26 hundred vehicles per hour, the other roads through town constrict the flow to a maximum of 23 hundred vehicles per hour. This can best be seen by considering lines across the network as shown above which cut the town in two, and the total capacity of the roads they cut. The minimum cut corresponds to the maximum flow.

71 1089 and the rest!

With four-digit numbers, *abcd*, the final sum is normally either 10 890 or 9999, depending on the differences $(a - b)$ and $(b - c)$, as the following analysis shows.

Assume $a > d$ ($a = d$ is a special case).

Then $(abcd - dcba)$ is equivalent to:

$(1000a + 100b + 10c + d) - (1000d + 100c + 10b + a)$
$= 999(a - d) + 90(b - c)$

Let $(a - d) = n$ and $(b - c) = m$, where $1 \le n \le 9$ and $1 \le m \le 9$.

Then $abcd - dcba = 999n + 90m$
$\qquad\qquad\qquad = 1000n + 100(m - 1) + 10(9 - m) + (10 - n)$
$\qquad\qquad\qquad = n\ (m - 1)\ (9 - m)\ (10 - n)$ On adding this to the numbers found by reversing its digits:

$\quad (10 - n)\ (9 - m)\ (m - 1)\ n$

we get the total 10 890

If $c > b$, let $(b - c) = -m$ where $1 \le m \le 9$.

Then $abcd - dcba = 999n - 90m$
$\qquad\qquad\qquad\quad =$
$1000(n - 1) + 100(10 - m) + 10(m - 1) + (10 - n)$
$\qquad\qquad\qquad = (n - 1)\ (10 - m)\ (m - 1)\ (10 - n)$

Reversing the digits and adding gives the total 9999.

When $b = c$, the resultant sum is 10 989.

With five-digit numbers, *abcde*, a very similar analysis occurs, As *abcde* − *edcba* cancels out the *c*-digit, the result depends only on $(a - e)$ and $(b - d)$.

The analysis for six-digit numbers follows similar lines.

72 A magical eye!

Here is one solution; now see how many of your own you can find.

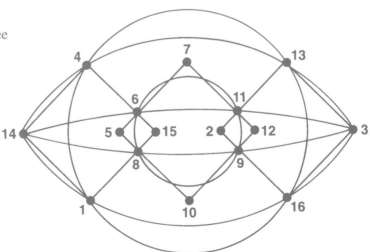

73 Devious Diana's dice

The adjoining table gives the differences which occur in the 36 ways in which two dice can land. It can be seen from this that 24 of these ways lead to 0, 1 or 2, while only 12 lead to 3, 4 or 5. It follows that the probability of Diana winning a throw is $\frac{2}{3}$ compared to Joe's $\frac{1}{3}$. The probability of Diana winning three consecutive throws is

	1	2	3	4	5	6
1	0	1	2	3	4	5
2	1	0	1	2	3	4
3	2	1	0	1	2	3
4	3	2	1	0	1	2
5	4	3	2	1	0	1
6	5	4	3	2	1	0

$\frac{2}{3} \times \frac{2}{3} \times \frac{2}{3} = \frac{8}{27}$, whilst the probability of Joe winning two consecutive throws is only $\frac{1}{3} \times \frac{1}{3} = \frac{1}{9} = \frac{3}{27}$.

So Diana's chance of winning 5p is almost three times as great as Joe's chance of winning 10p. She knew what she was doing!

74 Square sisters!

Anthea is 70 and Ena is 66

70: $1 + 2 + 5 + 7 + 10 + 14 + 35 + 70 = 144 = 12^2$
66: $1 + 2 + 3 + 6 + 11 + 22 + 33 + 66 = 144 = 12^2$

The factors of 94 also sum to 144, but this would mean that there was a very large age gap between the sisters.

75 Shunt your way out of this!

First let the goods engine G shunt itself into the siding; then let the passenger express P move past the siding with all its carriages. Then shunt G back onto the main line to the left of the siding. See figure (i).

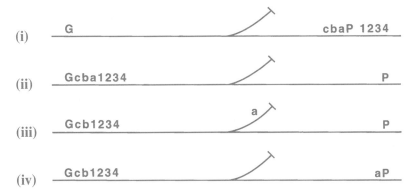

Now let the express train return to the left of the siding, then uncouple its engine and shunt it into the siding. G can now push the carriages along the main line and couple them with the goods wagons, then pull them all back to

the left of the siding, so allowing the express engine P to come out of the siding and move along the main line towards the port. See figure (ii)

G is then used to deposit wagons 1234 with P, shunt carriage a into the siding then returning to collect cb1234. See figure (iii).

Next G collects carriage a from the siding on the end of cb1234 and pushes it along the main line to connect with P. See figure (iv).

This sequence of operations is repeated twice more, first with carriage b going into the siding, and then carriage c going into the siding.

76 Map folding

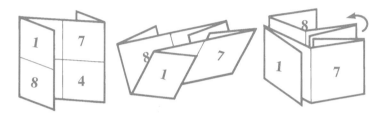

Fold the 1 and 8 forward in front of the 2 and 3, and the 6 and 5 backward behind the 7 and 4. Now fold along the middle horizontally so that 8 and 4 are at the back leaving just 1 and 7 visible in front. Finally, fold along the vertical and push the numbers on the right-hand side in between the 3 and 8 on the left-hand side.

77 Spot check!

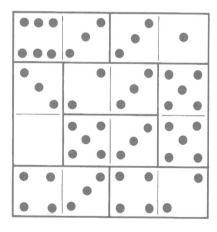

78 Neighbourliness!

One solution to each is given.

The idea for this puzzle came from Edward de Bono's book *The five-day course in thinking* (Pelican), which I recommend.

Now try placing eight cassette tape boxes so that each touches exactly five others.

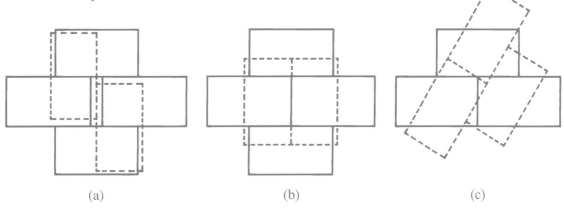

(a)   (b)   (c)

79 The communicative sisters

Only 8 calls are needed.

Suppose we call the six sisters A, B, C, D, E, F. Let: A phone B, B phone C, F phone E, E phone D, C phone D, B phone E, A phone C, F phone D, in that order. The following table indicates who the sisters know about after each phone call.

This solution is not unique. It can also be represented by a graph, where the sisters are represented by nodes and the phone calls by arcs. It is instructive to make a copy of this graph and mark in at each vertex the sisters known about after each call has been made.

You might like to investigate the number of phone calls required for different numbers of sisters, and generalise the results.

knows about	A	B	C	D	E	F
A	✓	1	7	7	7	7
B	1	✓	2	6	6	6
C	2	2	✓	5	5	5
D	5	5	5	✓	4	4
E	6	6	6	4	✓	3
F	8	8	8	8	3	✓

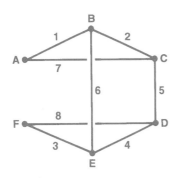

80 Marvellous '26'

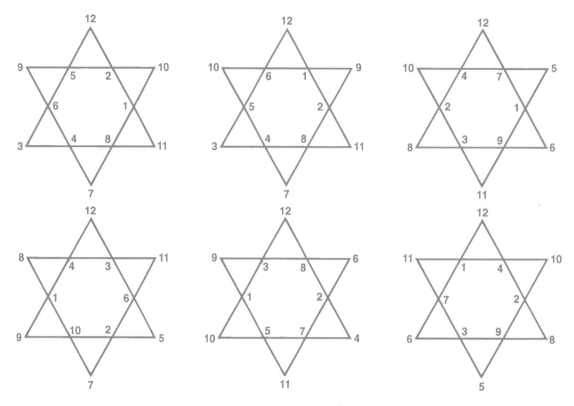

Shown here are the six entirely different arrangements which have totals of 26 along each side of the triangle and around the interior hexagon.

But let us examine the first solution more closely. In addition to the seven sets already mentioned:

(i) the three numbers at the vertices of the two large triangles also total 26: $3+12+11$ $9+10+7$

(ii) the five numbers forming the angles of the large triangles each total 26:
$6+5+12+2+1$ $5+2+10+1+8$ $2+1+11+8+4$,
$1+8+7+4+6$ $8+4+3+6+5$ $4+6+9+5+2$

(iii) the five numbers forming a pair of angles of the hexagon
$3+6+5+2+10$ and $3+4+8+1+10$,
together with the three numbers forming their vertically opposite angles
$9+5+12$ and $7+8+11$
also total '26'.

This gives a total of 19 ways but falls short of the 30 suggested by the originator of the game. Help!

Readers may like to read a short article on this game by Michael Cornelius in *Mathematics Teaching*, Vol. 120, September 1987, and may also find his book *Board Games Round the World* (Cambridge University Press) of interest.

81 Anna's Christmas shopping

7.5 dollars, 1.66 dollars, 0.8 dollars

In general, $abc = a + b + c$ if $c = (a + b) / (ab - 1)$

82 Alphabetic arithmetic!

This problem was first set by the author in 1958 in The Mathematical Gazette when he was a trainee teacher!

$$\frac{1}{10} = \frac{1}{11} + \frac{1}{110} = \frac{1}{12} + \frac{1}{60} = \frac{1}{14} + \frac{1}{35}$$

$$= \frac{1}{13} + \frac{1}{65} + \frac{1}{130} = \frac{1}{15} + \frac{1}{31} + \frac{1}{930}$$

$$= \frac{1}{16} + \frac{1}{40} + \frac{1}{80} = \frac{1}{17} + \frac{1}{34} + \frac{1}{85}$$

$$= \frac{1}{18} + \frac{1}{30} + \frac{1}{90} = \frac{1}{20} + \frac{1}{21} + \frac{1}{420}$$

This solution was sent in by Donald Cross, who later became a colleague at Exeter School of Education.

83 Who won?

Under system X the teams tie with 44 points each.
Under system Y Barchester wins by 26 points to 22.
Under system Z Athlone wins by 50 points to 46.

This should make you question the results of any sport using a points-scoring system!

84 How old are they?

There are two possible solutions:

Arthur 84, Brian 48, Christopher 12
Arthur 63, Brian 36, Christopher 9

85 In-flight refuelling

One tanker can be used to refuel the second tanker and the fighter, leaving them when it has filled their tanks and has just enough fuel to get back to base. Suppose this happens x miles into the flight, then the initial 4200 mile fuel load of the tanker has to be equivalent to 3x tanker miles and x fighter miles (equivalent to $\frac{1}{2}x$ tanker miles), giving

$$3x + \tfrac{1}{2}x = 4200$$

from which $\quad x = 1200$ miles

Now the second tanker and fighter fly on another y miles to the point where the fighter flies off alone with a full tank and the tanker has sufficient fuel to return to base. This is expressed by the equation:

$$2y + \tfrac{1}{2}y + 1200 = 4200$$

giving $\quad\quad y = 1200$ miles

Hence the range for the fighter is:

$$1200 + 1200 + 2000 = \textbf{4400 miles}$$

86 All scores equal!

The common score was 42.

Alan: 11 11 11 3 3 3
Ben: 11 11 7 7 3 3
Cheryl: 11 7 7 7 7 3
Denise: 7 7 7 7 7 7

87 The dinner party

Only one order satisfies all the criteria apart from being clockwise or anticlockwise. See the diagram where 'A' stands for Mr Allnight, 'a' for Mrs Allnight, and so on.

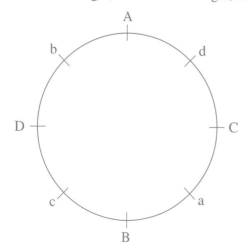

88 Mind reading!

The trick depends on the fact that if the digit sum of a number is divisible by 9 then so is the number itself. The sequence of operations carried out by the person with the calculator automatically produces a final result which is divisible by 9, so its digit sum must be divisible by 9, hence the method to find the missing digit.

Suppose the original number was x, then multiplying by 10 and subtracting itself gives $10x - x = 9x$, which is clearly divisible by 9. Now adding any number to it which is divisible by 9, such as 234, gives another number divisible by 9, hence the trick.

It follows that the trick would work with any size of initial number and the addition, or subtraction for that matter, of any number whose digit sum was divisible by 9.

89 Optimising transport costs

	P	Q	R	S
A	0	7	0	2
B	0	0	3	3
C	5	0	0	3

	P	Q	R	S
A	0	7	0	2
B	3	0	3	0
C	2	0	0	6

This is an example of an important problem in the application of mathematics known as 'The Transportation Problem'. There are algorithms for solving it but here it is expected that you make intelligent use of trial and error.

One strategy which often leads to a good solution, is to take the cheapest route first, then the next cheapest, and so on. This leads to the redistribution in the first table above with a cost of £850. However this uses the most expensive route BS for 3 cars and it is best avoided. The optimum solution is found by modifying this by changing by $+3$, -3, $+3$ and -3, the numbers of cars along BP, BS, CS and CP. This gives a total cost of £790.

For further reading on this type of problem read, for example, *An Introduction to Linear Programming and the Theory of Games* by S. Vajda (Methuen/Wiley) or *Mathematics in Management* by A. Battersby (Pelican) or *Decision Mathematics* by the Spode Group (Ellis Horwood).

90 Pentagonal magic!

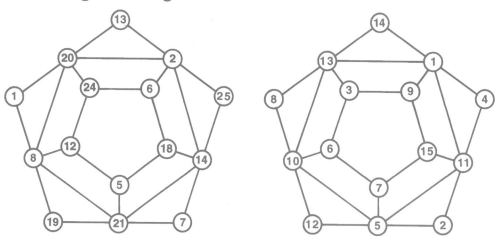

The solution to the given pentagon and one solution using the numbers 1 to 15 are shown. The solution using 1 to 15 was found by G. Corris, a teacher from Millfield School, after I challenged an audience at a sixth-form lecture to find it. Another solution can be found by using the transformation $n \to 16-n$, but are there any others? If there are, the magic total will, of necessity, be 40. Why?

91 Squaring up with 1 to 9

The following solutions were based on considering the squares of 1 to 50. By considering the squares of higher numbers you will find further solutions.

(a) 1 9   25   36 784
(b) 9 25   361 784
    1 36   529 784
    9 81   324 576
(c) 25 784 1369
    25 784 1936

The search for solutions is made easier by appreciating that the last digit of a square number must be one of the set 1, 4, 5, 6 and 9. Furthermore, in looking at the squares of the first 50 numbers only 4 of those which can be used contain the digit '7', namely 576, 729, 784 and 1764.

93 Find that angle!

Angle CDE = 50°

This problem first came to my attention when it was proposed by Masaaki Takahashi in the February 1991 issue of the Mathematical Society of Brunei Darussalam Newsletter.

Since then I have returned to it on many occasions and improved on my trigonometrical solution, which was based on several applications of the Sine Rule. But a Euclidean solution eluded me. In December 1993 I passed the problem to colleagues in the University of Exeter Mathematics Department and was delighted when Robin Chapman came up with the following very neat proof.

Construct *GE* and *EH*, where *AG* = *AE*, and *AH* = *AE*. This makes triangle *AGE* isosceles and triangle *AEH* equilateral.

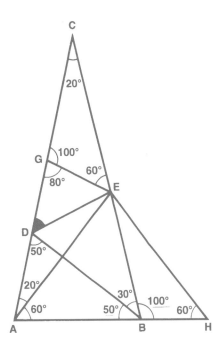

Step 1
Using the angle sum of a triangle and the sum of the angles on a straight line, we can quickly deduce that
angle *ACB* = 20°, angle *AGE* = 80°, angle *GEC* = 60°,
angle *ADB* = 50° and angle *EBH* = 100°

Step 2
Triangles *CGE* and *EBH* are now congruent, for their angles are equal and *CE* = *EH*, as *CE* = *AE* (triangle *AEC* is isosceles).

Step 3
    AD = *AB* (isosceles triangle)
    AG = *AH* (by construction)
so *DG* = *BH* (by subtraction)
but *GE* = *BH* (from the above congruence)
so *DG* = *GE*
Hence triangle *DGE* is isosceles and angle *GDE* = 50°

94 Jigsaw conjectures

106 edge pieces
   This puzzle is based on my own experience. I had to make the assumption that the jigsaw pieces were all approximately the same size and as high as they were wide. Then if there are $24x$ edge pieces along the bottom of the jigsaw, there will be $17x$ pieces up its sides. So $24x \times 17x \approx 736$. This leads to $x \approx 1.3431$, and the number of pieces along the edges being 32 and 23, confirmed by $32 \times 23 = 736$. All you need to remember now is that the corner pieces count twice, so the total number of edge pieces is $32 + 32 + 23 + 23 - 4 = 106$.
   Try generalising the result for any shape and size of rectangular jigsaw with N pieces.

95 Wayward's new coinage system!

Use 1Fk, 4Fk and 5Fk to obtain 1Fk to 15Fk
Use 1Fk, 4Fk, 7Fk and 8Fk to obtain 1Fk to 24Fk.
Using 1FK, 4Fk, 6Fk, 14Fk, and 15Fk, it is possible to
obtain all the totals to 36Fk.

The idea for this puzzle came from *Puzzle Tales* by
Martin Gardner (Penguin Books), where the idea is
extended and references for further reading can be found.

96 Ibrahim's tile torment!

Ibrahim would need 192 hexagonal tiles or 256 diamond tiles.

As the tiles each have the same perimeter, the ratio of the
lengths of the sides of the tiles are:

triangle:hexagon:diamond $= 1 : \frac{1}{2} : \frac{3}{4}$

So the areas of the triangles which make up the tiles are
in the ratio of the square of these ratios, namely:

$1 : \frac{1}{4} : \frac{9}{16}$

and the areas of the tiles will be in the ratio:

$1 : \frac{6}{4} : \frac{18}{16}$

or more simply $8 : 12 : 9$.

97 How large are the circles?

The small circle has radius $\frac{6}{23}$ cm and the larger one has
radius 6 cm.

The line joining the centres of two circles passes through
their point of contact so its length is the sum of their radii.
Hence triangle ABC is a $3:4:5$ triangle and right-angled.
Let the inner circle have centre D and radius r; then
$DA = r + 3$, $DB = r + 2$ and $DC = r + 1$. Take a Cartesian
frame of reference with C as the origin, CA as the x-axis,
and CB as the y-axis. If D has coordinates (x,y), then:

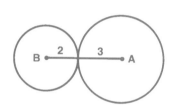

$$AD^2 = (4-x) + y^2 = (r+3)^2 \quad \text{①}$$
$$BD^2 = x^2 + (3-y)^2 = (r+2)^2 \quad \text{②}$$
$$CD^2 = x^2 + y^2 = (r+1)^2 \quad \text{③}$$

Taking ③ from ① leads to $2x = 2 - r$, and
taking ③ from ② leads to $3y = 3 - r$.

Substituting for x and y in terms of r from these last
two results gives the quadratic equation:

$23r^2 + 132r - 36 = 0$

which factorises to give:

$(23r - 6)(r + 6) = 0$

from which we get $r = \frac{6}{23}$

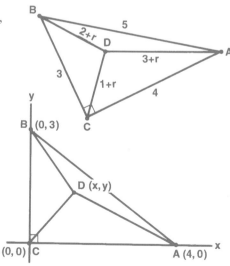

It is soon seen that if R is the radius of the enclosing circle, then the same approach as above leads to the equation $23R^2 - 132R - 36 = 0$, with factors $(23R + 6)$ and $(R - 6)$, which gives $R = 6$.

98 Packing perfume profitably

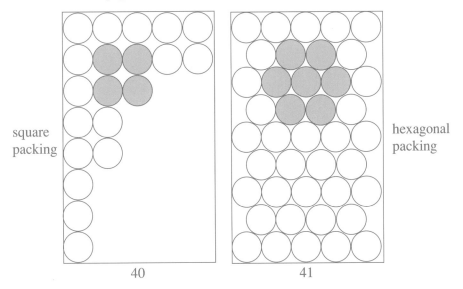

square packing

hexagonal packing

40   41

The extra bottle is achieved by using hexagonal packing instead of square packing. The smallest box of bottles using square packing which could be arranged in hexagonal packing to gain one bottle is one with 40 bottles in an 8×5 array.

This can be rearranged to hold 41 bottles. So Hex Agonal needs to buy 41 boxes of perfume.

The box packed with 40 and 41 bottles is shown here.

The key to solving this problem is to work out the distances between the lines of the centres of the bottles using hexagonal packing.

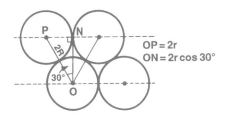

$OP = 2r$
$ON = 2r \cos 30°$

If the radius of a bottle is r, then the required distance is: $2r \cos 30° \approx r\sqrt{3} \approx 1.732r$

So the 9 rows in the hexagonal packing require a length of $r + 8 \times 1.732r + r \approx 15.856r$ which is less than the $16r$ of the square packing.

There are possibilities here for an interesting investigation into the number of circles which can be packed into different sizes of rectangle, and the efficiency of the packing measured as the percentage of the area of the rectangle occupied by the circles.

99 Primeval magic!

Every prime number greater than 3 is of the form $6n+1$ or $6n-1$, which is easily seen by writing the numbers in 6 columns as shown. The 2nd, 4th and 6th columns contain only even numbers while the 3rd column contains only multiples of 3, so none of these are prime except 2 and 3. The prime numbers are thus contained in the 1st and 5th columns which contain only numbers of the form $6n+1$ and $6n-1$.

1	2	3	4	5	6
7	8	9	10	11	12
13	14	15	16	17	18
19	20	21	22	23	24
25	26	27	28	29	30

Now $(6n+1)^2 = 36n^2 + 12n + 1$,

and $(6n-1)^2 = 36n^2 - 12n + 1$

so their remainder on division by 12 will always be 1. Adding 32 which leaves a remainder of 8 on division by 12 means the remainder of the process described will be $1 + 8 = 9$. The figures after the decimal point come from $\frac{9}{12} = 0.75$. By asking your friend to add numbers other than 32 to the square of his prime you can control the remainder to be any number from 0 to 11.

100 Golfing gymnastics!

Imagine the ten boxes labelled A, B, C, D, E, F, G, H, I, J.

Take 1 ball from A, 2 from B, 3 from C, 4 from D, 5 from E, and balance them against 1 from F, 2 from G, 3 from H, 4 from I, and 5 from J, by using as many gram weights as needed. The number of grams required, and which pan they are needed in, tells you immediately which box has the light, substandard balls.

For example, suppose 3 grams are needed in the first pan then that side must have been 3 grams too light which implies that box C contains the substandard balls. If I had been the substandard box, then 4 grams would have been needed in the second pan to achieve a balance.

This solution neatly sorts out the rogue box, but Sidney could well be left wondering which of the balls on his scale pan are faulty!

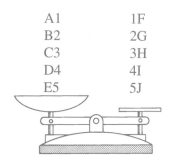

```
A1        1F
B2        2G
C3        3H
D4        4I
E5        5J
```

101 A sixth-order difference triangle

This is the only possible solution for any 21 numbers from the set 1, 2, 3, ... 22, See puzzle 41 for references.

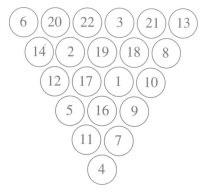

102 Grandfather's deliberations!

Professor Integer: 88; son: 55; granddaughters: 21, 8, 3, 1.

To find the smallest number which cannot be expressed as the sum of fewer than five different Fibonacci numbers, you need to take the five alternate Fibonacci numbers starting with 1 and 3.

103 Triangulation?

The builder was wrong in assuming that the site was a triangle. The slope of the triangles is different – not by a lot, but enough to make a significant difference in the area.

104 Circles into squares!

With 3 coins the best arrangement is to have them all touching each other with one in the corner of the square and the other two placed symmetrically about the diagonal. The side of the square is then of length

$$2R + 2R\cos 15° \approx 3.932R$$

which is almost as large as the square containing 4 coins.

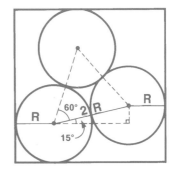

The solution for 5 coins is straightforward, with the coins along the diagonals as shown. The side of the square now has length:

$$2R + 4R\cos 45° \approx 4.828R$$

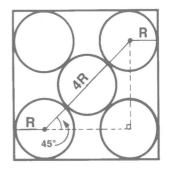

The solution for 6 coins is not so obvious, see the diagram. The coins are placed at such an angle θ, that they touch the sides of the square. For this to happen their height, $2R + 6R\sin\theta$, must equal their width, $2R + 4R\cos\theta$. So $2R + 6R\sin\theta = 2R = 4R\cos\theta$ from which $\tan\theta = \frac{2}{3}$, giving $\theta \approx 33.69°$ and the square of side $5.328R$.

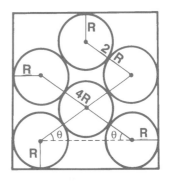

The solution for 7 coins appears wasteful of space, but cannot be bettered, see the diagram. The square has side:
$$4R + 2R\cos 30° \approx 5.732R.$$

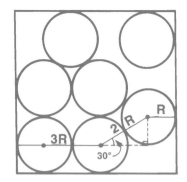

The solution for 8 coins is closely related to that for 3 coins in the way the groups of 3 fit into each corner of the square. In this case the length of side of the square is
$$2R + 4R\cos 15° = 5.864R.$$

Now you have seen these solutions you can investigate the optimum way to pack larger numbers of coins into squares.

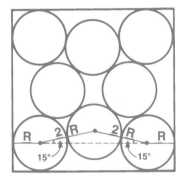

105 Minimising manpower!

The best solution to this puzzle has been sent to me by Maurice Godfrey from Millfield School and requires only 21 porters. This is achieved by setting out with provisions for 204 person-days and sending back: 3 porters after 1 day, 3 porters after 2 days, 2 porters after 3 days, 3 porters after 4 days, and 3 porters after 5 days, leaving 7 porters to continue for the next 7 days.

To get a feel for the problem it helps to consider how far the explorers could get if no porters returned to base. Suppose they start out with n porters then they will be starting with 10n person-days of supplies for $n + 3$ people, so they will be able to trek for L days given by the formula:

$$L = \frac{10n}{n + 3}$$ and the following table gives some data from

using it:

n	2	3	5	7	12	27	97
L	4	5	6.25	7	8	9	9.7

Clearly, no matter how large a number of porters the explorers start with they can never manage even a 10-day trek unless some return at an early stage.

If only one returning group is used then they must do so after day 3 or day 4, for the remaining group can at best support themselves and the explorers for 9 days as the table above shows.

If the returning group goes back after 3 days then 50 porters are needed, of whom 23 return. But if the returning group does so after 4 days then only 42 porters are needed of whom 30 return.

Other solutions are possible using 21 porters, but they are not so economical as they require that the party start out with provisions for more than 204 person-days. The alternative solutions, all due to Maurice Godfrey and his computer, can be summarised as:

21/206/3, 2, 3, 3, 3   21/206/2, 4, 2, 3, 3

21/208/2, 3, 3, 3, 3   21/210/2, 3, 3, 3, 2

106 The chain challenge

1025 gives the longest chain, with 21 steps.

A chain formed mainly of even numbers such as:

$96 \to 48 \to 24 \to 12 \to 6 \to 3 \to 4 \to 2 \to 1$

reduces in size very quickly as the number is frequently halved. To slow down the rate of descent we need to introduce as many odd numbers in the chain as possible. The best that can be achieved is for every other number in the chain to be odd. The easiest way to find the chain is to start at 1 and work backwards. An odd number must come from its double and we let the resulting even number come from the odd number which is 1 less than itself. This gives the chain:

1, 2, 4, 3, 6, 5, 10, 9, 18, 17, 34, 33, 66, 65, 130, 129, 258, 257, 514, 513, 1026, 1025

107 Reflections in their prime!

This should not be difficult to solve as Emily's age must be the square of an odd number for the numbers 2 each side of it to be prime. This soon leads to their ages being 83, 81 and 79, so they were born in 1914, 1916 and 1918 respectively. The only other Christmas when their ages had similar properties was in 1925 when they were 11, 9 and 7. They were all prime in 1921 when their ages were 7, 5 and 3.

108 Every triangle is isosceles

Unless you make a careful drawing you will probably remain baffled! The intersection of the angle bisector and the perpendicular bisector, X lies outside the triangle and R and Q lie so that one is inside and the other outside the triangle.

109 What comes next?

(a) This sequence is generated by alternately multiplying by 2 and adding 5, so the next two terms are 102 and 107.

(b) This sequence is formed by alternately squaring and subtracting 1, so the next two terms are 3969 and 3968.

(c) If prime add 2, if not prime add 1, so the next two terms are 15 and 16.

110 Pipe packing

When two pipes of radii R and r are placed side by side on a horizontal surface the horizontal distance between their centres can easily be calculated using Pythagoras' theorem: $d^2 = (R + r)^2 - (R - r)^2$

$$= 4Rr$$
$$\text{so } d = 2\sqrt{(Rr)}$$

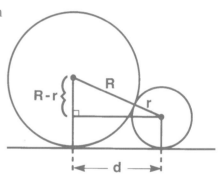

Using this formula the following table can be constructed giving the horizontal distances between the centres of the different sizes of pipes when placed next to each other.

	8	5	3	2
10	$2\sqrt{80}$	$2\sqrt{50}$	$2\sqrt{30}$	$2\sqrt{20}$
8		$2\sqrt{40}$	$2\sqrt{24}$	$2\sqrt{16}$
5			$2\sqrt{15}$	$2\sqrt{10}$
3				$2\sqrt{6}$

An examination of this table suggests the best savings are achieved by placing small diameter pipes next to large ones. In fact the manager's solution would give the worst possible packing, requiring a crate with an internal width of:

$$10 + 2(\sqrt{80} + \sqrt{40} + \sqrt{15} + \sqrt{6}) + 4 + 2 = 59.183 \text{ cm}$$

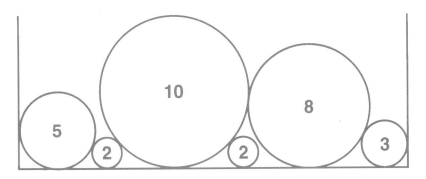

The best solution found so far is due to Prof. Yoshio Kimura, with the order 5, 2, 10, 2, 8, 3. In this case, the pipes with radii 10 cm and 8 cm touch each other, leaving more than enough space for a 2 cm radius pipe between them. This solution requires a crate with internal width:

$$5 + 2(\sqrt{10} + \sqrt{20} + \sqrt{80} + \sqrt{24}) + 3 = 50.955 \text{ cm}$$

This solution, of course, ignores the possibility of packing pipes within pipes!

111 Prof. Nilfactor's telephone number!

The number is 73 939 133
    Other 8-digit numbers with the required property are:
    23 399 339   29 399 999   37 337 999   59 393 339

Feel pleased with yourself if you found any of them! A calculator and a table of prime numbers will only take you so far. What you need is a micro computer with a program for testing whether or not a number is prime.
    A detailed discussion of these numbers is to be found in Activity 43. 'Truncating primes', in *Even more mathematical activities* by Brian Bolt, (Cambridge University Press).

112 Elliptical areas

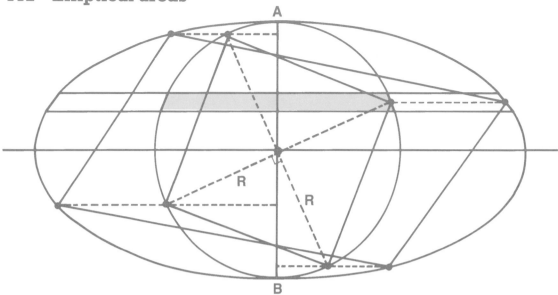

(a) The area bounded by the circle and any two adjacent parallel lines is approximately a trapezium, and under the stretching process its area is doubled. By imagining the circle stretched to the ellipse by using say, 100 parallel lines, you can see that all the thin trapezia into which the circle is divided get doubled in the area to form the ellipse. So the area of the ellipse is twice the area of the circle, that is $2\pi R^2$. More generally, if the circle was stretched by a factor k, then the resulting ellipse would have area $k\pi R^2$.

(b) The largest quadrilateral which can be drawn in the circle is a square of area $2R^2$, and area of the largest quadrilateral possible in the ellipse is the parallelogram resulting from stretching such a square by a scale factor of 2 at right-angles to AOB as shown in the diagram, with area $4R^2$.

113 Matrix voyages:

Two other matrix manipulators which enable the traveller to visit all 8 points are $\begin{pmatrix} 0 & 1 \\ 1 & 1 \end{pmatrix}, \begin{pmatrix} 1 & 1 \\ 1 & 0 \end{pmatrix}$ but there are others.

The matrices $\begin{pmatrix} 4 & 3 \\ 2 & 2 \end{pmatrix}, \begin{pmatrix} 1 & 1 \\ 1 & 3 \end{pmatrix}, \begin{pmatrix} 1 & 1 \\ 3 & 1 \end{pmatrix}$ and $\begin{pmatrix} 1 & 3 \\ 1 & 1 \end{pmatrix}$ all take a traveller

around the 24 points, other than the origin, of the 25-point world.

Try investigating other finite worlds such as:

(a) the two-dimensional world of 16 points: (0,0) to
(3,3) where you use modulo 4 arithmetic.

(b) the three-dimensional world of 27 points with
coordinates $(0,0,0,)$ to $(2,2,2)$ where the matrix
manipulators will be 3×3 and the operations in
modulo 3 arithmetic.

How about a four-dimensional world with the 16 points $(0,0,0,0)$
to $(1,1,1,1)$ using 4×4 matrices and modulo 2 arithmetic!

114   The surprising sphere

The sphere has a radius of 9, and its centre is $(10, 10, 10)$.

There are 102 different points on its surface whose coordinates
are all positive. The four points given are the key to all the
alternatives.

The vectors from the centre to each of the points must have
integer components and be of length 9. These are based on the four
vectors:

$$\begin{pmatrix} 9 \\ 0 \\ 0 \end{pmatrix} \begin{pmatrix} 7 \\ 4 \\ 4 \end{pmatrix} \begin{pmatrix} 3 \\ 6 \\ 6 \end{pmatrix} \begin{pmatrix} 8 \\ 4 \\ 1 \end{pmatrix} \quad \begin{aligned} 7^2 + 4^2 + 4^2 &= 81 \\ 3^2 + 6^2 + 6^2 &= 81 \\ 8^2 + 4^2 + 1^2 &= 81 \end{aligned}$$

From the first of these, by varying the position of the 9 and
introducing negative signs, 6 points can be found by adding the
following vectors in turn to $(10, 10, 10)$:

$$\begin{pmatrix} 9 \\ 0 \\ 0 \end{pmatrix} \begin{pmatrix} -9 \\ 0 \\ 0 \end{pmatrix} \begin{pmatrix} 0 \\ 9 \\ 0 \end{pmatrix} \begin{pmatrix} 0 \\ -9 \\ 0 \end{pmatrix} \begin{pmatrix} 0 \\ 0 \\ 9 \end{pmatrix} \begin{pmatrix} 0 \\ 0 \\ -9 \end{pmatrix}$$

Using the second, there are 3 positions to put the 7, and for each
of these ways there are 8 ways of distributing negative signs or not,
giving 24 ways in all. One set of 8 is shown below:

$$\begin{pmatrix} 7 \\ 4 \\ 4 \end{pmatrix} \begin{pmatrix} -7 \\ 4 \\ 4 \end{pmatrix} \begin{pmatrix} 7 \\ -4 \\ 4 \end{pmatrix} \begin{pmatrix} 7 \\ 4 \\ -4 \end{pmatrix} \begin{pmatrix} 7 \\ -4 \\ -4 \end{pmatrix} \begin{pmatrix} -7 \\ 4 \\ -4 \end{pmatrix} \begin{pmatrix} -7 \\ -4 \\ 4 \end{pmatrix} \begin{pmatrix} -7 \\ -4 \\ -4 \end{pmatrix}$$

Similarly, there are 24 different vectors which can be generated
by the components of the third vector. The fourth vector has the
three different components 8, 4 and 1, and these can be permuted in
6 ways before introducing negatives which multiplies the possible
alternatives by 8, giving 48 ways in all from this starting point!

Hence the total number of points is

$$6 + 24 + 24 + 48 = 102$$